I love finding new treasures in Scripture, fu[...] familiar and ordinary verses. By uncoveri[...] and allusions original readers would notice, Michael Williams shares some of these gems with us, reinvigorating our time in Scripture with the sparkle of God's glory.

AIMEE BYRD, author of *The Sexual Reformation* and
Recovering from Biblical Manhood and Womanhood

Michael Williams brings out the "hidden depths" of thirty Old Testament passages by careful attention to context and the details of the passage. He is not discovering some secret meaning, but rather brings out the surprising dimensions of the passage he is so skillfully reading. Written in an accessible and winsome style, this book is recommended for all lovers of the Bible.

TREMPER LONGMAN III, PhD, distinguished scholar
and professor emeritus of Biblical Studies, Westmont College

Michael Williams masters technical Old Testament scholarship and makes it accessible to the ordinary layperson. He understands how Old Testament passages point to Christ and apply to believers today. His deeper meanings are neither allegorical nor idiosyncratic but highlight what the original authors intended with the words they chose. He reinforces his interpretations with memorable puns himself. This book could be used in the classroom or for devotions but will enjoyably inform many other readers as well. Countless thanks to Williams for these valuable insights!

CRAIG L. BLOMBERG, distinguished professor
emeritus of New Testament, Denver Seminary

What does the church (and our world) need more than ever? Deeper discipleship from understanding the Bible and living in light of God's Word. Michael Williams is a gifted Bible scholar and teacher with a passion for all believers to understand the faithfulness of God by seeing how even one verse in Scripture can help a person see the bigger picture of God's grace. Through short but penetrating studies of thirty Old Testament texts, we are given a tour of the Old Testament to see the wider frame for understanding the scope of God's care for us. With clarity and compassion, Williams makes sure that all readers gain confidence in trusting that the God who makes his promises known has kept those promises through all generations. Enjoy this journey!

JUL MEDENBLIK, president of Calvin Theological Seminary

In this work of careful scholarship, the author's goal is not to surface a meaning different from traditional understandings but a deeper meaning, thus enhancing the meaning. The treatment of these selected passages is balanced, thorough, and well reasoned. The author provides examples of how to enhance the semantic range of the texts he discusses. My heartfelt appreciation and congratulations go to Michael Williams.

KENNETH L. BARKER, general editor, *NIV Study Bible*

Michael Williams writes a gem of a book showing how "ordinary" Old Testament moments have more to teach us than we might suspect. He shines a light on thirty passages, taking a closer look at their contexts. Historical insights joined with close attention to the details of the text bring these passages to life in new ways. *30 Old Testament Passages with Deeper Meaning* is as engaging as it is accessible. I highly recommend it.

JEANNINE K. BROWN, Bethel
Seminary, Saint Paul, Minnesota

Michael Williams is a highly perceptive reader of the Bible, and his insights into it are sharp and penetrating. But he wears his rich learning lightly and writes so clearly so that we can readily absorb his fine teaching. This book is a gift.

CORNELIUS PLANTINGA, author
of *Under the Wings of God*

An illuminating exploration of thirty remarkable Old Testament texts by a master teacher. Each chapter provides an entry point into not only a single verse's meaning but to larger dimensions of the worldview and culture reflected in the Hebrew scriptures. The book is accessible to all and will also inspire teachers who seek to translate insights from advanced theological study for wide audiences.

JOHN D. WITVLIET, Calvin Institute of Christian Worship

30
Old Testament Passages with Deeper Meaning

30
OLD TESTAMENT PASSAGES WITH DEEPER MEANING

The Surprising Significance
of Seemingly Ordinary Verses

MICHAEL WILLIAMS

ZONDERVAN

30 Old Testament Passages with Deeper Meaning
Copyright © 2023 by Michael Williams

Requests for information should be addressed to:
Zondervan, *3900 Sparks Dr. SE, Grand Rapids, Michigan 49546*

Zondervan titles may be purchased in bulk for educational, business, fundraising, or sales promotional use. For information, please email SpecialMarkets@Zondervan.com.

ISBN 978-0-310-14434-2 (audio)

Library of Congress Cataloging-in-Publication Data
Names: Williams, Michael James, 1956– author.
Title: 30 Old Testament passages with deeper meaning : the surprising significance of seemingly ordinary verses / Michael Williams.
Other titles: Bible. Old Testament. Selections. English. 2023. | Thirty Old Testament passages with deeper meaning
Description: Grand Rapids : Zondervan, 2023. | Includes bibliographical references.
Identifiers: LCCN 2022052928 (print) | LCCN 2022052929 (ebook) | ISBN 9780310144328 (paperback) | ISBN 9780310144335 (ebook)
Subjects: LCSH: Bible. Old Testament—Quotations. | Bible. Old Testament—Criticism, interpretation, etc. | Bible. Old Testament—Use. | BISAC: RELIGION / Biblical Studies / Old Testament / Historical Books | RELIGION / Biblical Reference / Quotations
Classification: LCC BS1091 .W8 2023 (print) | LCC BS1091 (ebook) | DDC 221.5/2—dc23/eng/20221230
LC record available at https://lccn.loc.gov/2022052928
LC ebook record available at https://lccn.loc.gov/2022052929

Cover design: Thinkpen Design
Cover photo: © Isaac Davis / Unsplash
Interior design: Sara Colley

Printed in the United States of America

23 24 25 26 27 28 29 30   /TRM/   14 13 12 11 10 9 8 7 6 5 4 3 2 1

Contents

ACKNOWLEDGMENTS

There could be no exploration of the deeper meaning of Old Testament passages if there were no deeper meaning there to be explored in the first place. The reason it *is* there, of course, is because our Lord has put it there. And he has communicated to us these amazingly interconnected, unfathomably deep, and profound Scriptures that reflect his divine genius. He has also given us minds that can begin to access these rich treasures. Acknowledgement of these truths must be the starting point for our efforts at understanding the Bible and also forces a realization that such an investigation will never be exhausted because of the inability of our created minds to fully comprehend the mind of our Creator, even though we have been fashioned in a way that makes it irresistible and necessary for us to try.

I must acknowledge with appreciation the extremely helpful people at Zondervan who have encouraged me to pursue these explorations into deeper meanings of Old Testament passages. Nancy Erickson gave me the green light to proceed when I first presented the idea and has been a constant champion of making scholarship accessible to the broader church. Dale Williams (no relation, though sharing a noble surname) enthusiastically received the proposal and has made the entire behind-the-scenes process of shepherding it to publication hum along like a well-oiled machine. My appreciation extends as well to the dedicated sales professionals of HCCP who work so hard to get books like this one into the hands of readers everywhere. I could not have hoped to work with more supportive and encouraging people.

There is one person, however, who rises above all other mortals as my muse, support, counselor, exemplar, best friend, and soul mate—Dawn, my wife of thirty-eight years. It is one thing to explore the deeper meanings of scriptural passages in a book; it is quite another to see them lived out in practical life circumstances. Dawn continues to teach me what growth toward Christlikeness looks like. Any helpful suggestions for applying biblical truths found in this book have been deeply influenced by her grace-filled life. To her I say, "Many women do noble things, but you surpass them all" (Prov 31:29).

Resource
Abbreviations

AEL	*Ancient Egyptian Literature.* Miriam Lichtheim. 3 vols. Berkeley: University of California Press, 1971–1980.
AnBib	Analecta Biblica
ANET	*Ancient Near Eastern Texts Relating to the Old Testament.* Edited by James B. Pritchard. 3rd ed. Princeton: Princeton University Press, 1969.
BAR	*Biblical Archaeology Review*
BDB	Brown, Francis, S. R. Driver, and Charles A. Briggs. *A Hebrew and English Lexicon of the Old Testament.*
CAD	*The Assyrian Dictionary of the Oriental Institute of the University of Chicago.* Chicago: The Oriental Institute of the University of Chicago, 1956–2006.
CANE	*Civilizations of the Ancient Near East.* Edited by Jack M. Sasson. 4 vols. New York, 1995. Repr. in 2 vols. Peabody, MA: Hendrickson, 2006.
COED	*The Compact Oxford English Dictionary.* Oxford: Clarendon, 1991.

COS	*The Context of Scripture.* Edited by William W. Hallo. 3 vols. Leiden: Brill, 1997–2002.
CTA	*Corpus des tablettes en cunéiformes alphabétiques découvertes à Ras Shamra-Ugarit de 1929 à 1939.* Edited by Andrée Herdner. Paris: Geuthner, 1963.
DANE	*Dictionary of the Ancient Near East.* Edited by Piotr Bienkowski and Alan Millard. Philadelphia: University of Pennsylvania Press, 2000.
DBI	*Dictionary of Biblical Imagery.* Edited by Leland Ryken, James C. Wilhoit, and Tremper Longman III. Downers Grove, IL: InterVarsity Press, 1998.
EBC	*The Expositor's Bible Commentary.* Edited by Frank E. Gaebelein. 12 vols. Grand Rapids: Zondervan, 1976–1992.
EBCr	*The Expositor's Bible Commentary.* Rev. ed. Edited by Tremper Longman III and David E. Garland. 13 vols. Grand Rapids: Zondervan, 2006–2012.
EDT	*Evangelical Dictionary of Theology.* Edited by Walter E. Elwell. Grand Rapids: Baker Academic, 1984.
HALOT	*The Hebrew and Aramaic Lexicon of the Old Testament.* Ludwig Koehler, Walter Baumgartner, and Johann J. Stamm. Translated and edited under the supervision of Mervyn E. J. Richardson. 4 vols. Leiden: Brill, 1994–1999.
Historia	*Historia: Zeitschrift für alte Geschichte*
IDB	*The Interpreter's Dictionary of the Bible.* Edited by George A. Buttrick. 4 vols. New York: Abingdon, 1962.
JCS	*Journal of Cuneiform Studies*

LCL	Loeb Classical Library
NIB	*The New Interpreter's Bible.* Edited by Leander E. Keck, et al. 12 vols. Nashville: Abingdon, 1994–2004.
NIDOTTE	*New International Dictionary of Old Testament Theology and Exegesis.* Edited by Willem A. VanGemeren. 5 vols. Grand Rapids: Zondervan, 1997.
NIVAC	New International Version Application Commentary
RIDA	*Revue internationale des droits de l'antiquité*
ZIBBC	*Zondervan Illustrated Bible Backgrounds Commentary: Old Testament.* Edited by John H. Walton. 5 vols. Grand Rapids: Zondervan, 2009.

Diving into "Deeper Meaning"

By "deeper meaning" I am not suggesting a kind of secret meaning that has only recently come to light after the discovery of some forgotten manuscripts that had been crumbling away in a long-sealed storeroom of an ancient monastery situated atop a remote desert mountain. Nor am I suggesting a deeper meaning that can be discovered and deciphered only by the correct application of innovative processes, filters, or interpretive grids. Such "deeper" meanings are more the stuff of popular adventure novels or Hollywood movies that feature exotic characters or involve elaborate doomsday scenarios that can be averted only by acting on their cryptic messages.

Rather, what I mean is something far more realistic and far more accessible, and yet no less exciting! These deeper meanings lie waiting to be discovered just below the plain sense of many biblical texts. We may have read over these texts dozens of times and yet remain entirely unaware of the surprising significance they possess. If we pause for a few moments on such seemingly ordinary verses and appraise them from new angles and perspectives, we will find not a *different* meaning from that obtainable by a surface reading of the passage but a *deeper* meaning. That deeper meaning may have been obscured by a heavy layer of cultural and language differences, by the dust of historical distance, or by a loss of focus on the Bible's main theme, Jesus Christ. When this masking patina is wiped away, we will discover that the biblical passages we thought we knew have a new power and surprising significance that we never realized. We will come away from our reading with a reawakened appreciation for the treasure that has been given to us. It is a treasure whose true, greater value occasionally needs to be explained so that we can be sure to give it the attention, care, and respect it deserves.

The situation with these surprising verses is not unlike what is regularly encountered on the popular PBS series *Antiques Roadshow*. On each episode, people bring into the studio various items they have found lying around their homes that they suspect might have a significance beyond what they have recognized. They present these artifacts to specialists who, after careful examination of the items, provide their curious owners with accurate appraisals of their value and some of the history behind them. Without fail, on each episode people are shocked when they learn that an item they had regarded as ordinary but potentially interesting turns out to be worth tens, if not hundreds, of thousands of dollars! It might be a rare Persian rug that has been catching spills under the dining room table. Perhaps it is a sun-faded painting taken from a wall in the hallway that turns out to be a highly respected artist's missing masterpiece. It might even be supposed costume jewelry that turns out to be nothing of the sort but rather genuine gold or silver laden with precious gems. When the gobsmacked owners learn the true value of what they had previously only casually regarded, they treat their possessions with a new, profound respect. The surprises come from all parts of the country and from all sorts of people. The same is true with the many seemingly ordinary verses of the Bible. The verses come from all parts of the Bible, including the historical, wisdom, poetic, legal, and prophetic texts. And they come from all sorts of people, including Moses, judges, prophets, kings, sages, and—as we'll see—even people from non-Israelite cultures!

Of course, the greater depths of meaning these verses possess were no doubt noticed by their original readers and hearers. The expressions, allusions, wordplays, and other literary features in these verses would have been immediately recognized by, and grabbed the attention and interest of, God's people in biblical times. But time moves on. And just as the passing of time brings with it a fading awareness of the significance of those surprise treasures on *Antiques Roadshow,* so the passing of time unfortunately brings along with it a fading awareness of the significance of the biblical treasures as well. It is therefore time for us to bring some of these seemingly ordinary biblical verses in for reappraisal. When we reexamine these verses from new perspectives, we may very well be just as gobsmacked when we learn their surprising significance. We'll see that there is *so much more* depth to them than we could have imagined!

The Bible abounds with such verses, and there is simply not enough room in a book this size to consider them all. We must limit ourselves in some way. Because the verses that are the most culturally and chronologically remote from our contemporary circumstances (and therefore the verses whose deeper meaning is most likely to be overlooked) are found in the Old Testament, our explorations will be limited to these. But even restricting ourselves to the Old Testament yields too many verses to adequately consider. The biblical texts are so extensive and cover such a long period of time that we must pick and choose. Consequently, the verses we will investigate are not to be regarded as comprising a comprehensive list, nor are they structured in any formal way around specific topics or the kinds of deeper meaning they possess. Rather, the passages are arranged in their canonical order, enabling readers to easily access whatever section of the Bible they wish to explore further. And because these chapters do not build on each other, readers can delve into the deeper meaning of these passages in any order they choose.

The Bible is a bottomless reservoir of meaning. We are therefore limited not only in the scope of our investigation but also in the level of its detail. Readers who desire to investigate some of these details even more deeply can refer to the information and resources provided in the notes to each chapter, located at the end of the book. But no matter how deeply we explore these seemingly ordinary verses, we should never think we have exhausted all there is to say in each case regarding the biblical authors' inspired literary imagination and skill. We can always go deeper. We can always say, "But wait, there's more!" So let's begin exploring at least some of the "more" these verses have to offer us.

1

— ○ —

ONE OF THESE
THINGS IS NOT
LIKE THE OTHERS

*In the beginning God created the
heavens and the earth.*
—GENESIS 1:1

On the PBS television series *Sesame Street*, there is a well-known sketch that is immediately identifiable by its song, "One of These Things Is Not like the Others." Viewers are encouraged to notice how one item stands out as different from those around it. There may be many similar details, but the item we're encouraged to notice is dissimilar in some significant way. We don't have to go far into the Bible to encounter an analogous phenomenon. In fact, in the very first verse of the book of Genesis we find something that is unique among the creation stories (cosmogonies) of the ancient Near East. It is, one could say, the creation account that is not like the others. The Genesis account would certainly have caught people's attention because of its arresting difference. It is this difference that we explore here because it contains a remarkable significance that may not be obvious to the modern reader. The hidden depths of meaning revealed by such an exploration are a result of (1) this creation account's surprising departure from the theologies and philosophies of other cultures and (2) the way that departure is communicated by the content and even the form of the biblical story. So before we look more closely at the text of Genesis 1:1, we must turn our attention to the stories of Israel's neighbors to see what additional light they can shed on the biblical account by way of contrast.

We look first to Israel's southern neighbor, Egypt, where the Israelites resided for over four hundred years, most of which were spent in less-than-optimal conditions (Gen 15:13). Identifying a unified and consistent Egyptian mythology surrounding creation, however, is not as straightforward as we might have hoped. This is due to the different nuances introduced by the various religious centers in Egypt that speculated about and wrote on this topic. Jacobus van Dijk has helpfully summarized the confusing situation in Egypt: "Speculation on [cosmogony] mainly originated in the great religious centers of Heliopolis (biblical On), Memphis (biblical Noph, modern Mit Rahina), Hermopolis (modern al-Ashmunein), and Thebes. . . . Each school of thought further elaborated the train of speculation of the other, adding its own insights to it rather than replacing it."[1]

In light of the progressive changes to Egyptian conceptions of cosmogony, it is perhaps most helpful to focus on the foundational ideas originating in the city of Heliopolis because it was the source of "the cosmogony that provided the basis for all later speculations."[2] In the cosmogony of Heliopolis, the Egyptian creator-god, Atum, "floats in the Primeval Waters . . . and to a certain extent [is] identical with them."[3] Regarding the origin of Atum himself, in a papyrus dating from the Ramesside period (1292–1069 BC), we are told—in words that are admittedly conceptually confusing—that he is "the one who evolved as evolver."[4] His evolving or self-manifestation "brings about the gradual unfolding of undifferentiated unity into the differentiated diversity of the world as we know it."[5] In simpler terms, in the cosmogony of Heliopolis, all the details of creation are simply evolutions or self-generations of Atum. Thus, this ancient Egyptian cosmogony is essentially panentheism, the belief that God contains the entire universe within himself.

We find something similar when we turn our attention to the area northeast of Israel, to Babylonia, the region of Abraham's homeland. In the longest Babylonian cosmogony, composed at least as early as the second millennium BC, the primeval waters are again pictured as existing before anything else and as the primordial substance from which everything else, including the gods, emerged. In this account, entitled Enuma Elish (its first two words in Akkadian), the primeval waters are named Tiamat (usually understood to refer to saltwater) and Apsu (usually understood to refer to freshwater):

> When on high no name was given to heaven
> [i.e., it had not yet been created],
> nor below was the netherworld called by name,
> Primeval Apsu was their progenitor,

and matrix-Tiamat was she who bore them all,
They were mingling their waters together. . . .
Then were the gods formed within these two.[6]

These words clearly communicate that in the Babylonian cosmogony, just as in the Egyptian cosmogony, the source of all life, including that of the gods themselves, can be ultimately traced back to the primeval waters. Curiously, however, no explanation is provided regarding the origin of the waters themselves.

As in the Egyptian and Babylonian cosmogonies, the biblical account also includes chaotic primeval waters (Gen 1:2). But in the Bible these waters are not presented as the fertile source that somehow independently generates all life. Instead, in a drastic departure from the other ancient Near Eastern cosmogonies (the significant detail that is not like the others), we are told that these waters, along with everything else, are the creation of an eternally existing God who is distinct from them. This God creates everything not as a differentiation of himself in some process of self-evolution or as secondary creations following his own mysterious formation but as discrete components of a good creation that he speaks into existence. In other words, the surprising difference the biblical account presents to us at its very beginning is that the unique Creator is utterly distinct from his creation.

But wait, there's more! If we drill down even more deeply into the first verse of Genesis, we notice another way this absolute distinction between God and his creation is indicated. It is signaled by a seemingly insignificant orthographic feature of biblical Hebrew—the verse's accent marks! Biblical Hebrew has no punctuation marks such as are found in most of the world's languages. Instead, it uses accents to perform many of the functions of punctuation. Like hyphens, conjunctive accents are used to indicate words that are intended to be read together. And like commas, periods, or semicolons, disjunctive accents indicate words after which one should pause. Paying attention to these disjunctive accents can reveal to us where one thought ends in a verse and another begins. The Hebrew of Genesis 1:1 (and its English translation) is only one sentence, but in this single sentence we find an important disjunctive accent that indicates a major division of thought. The two halves of this verse, divided by this disjunctive accent, are therefore communicating two separate, distinct ideas. The first part of the verse is communicating the *who* of creation: *God* created. The second part of the verse is communicating the *what* of creation: *the heavens and the earth*. The very way this verse is written—using a disjunctive accent to divide its two thoughts—highlights the distinctiveness of the biblical creation account from all others in the ancient Near East: it is not the primeval waters that create the god (by means of some process of self-differentiation); it is God who creates the primeval waters (and everything else by his word).

If we consider the descriptions of these primeval waters a bit more closely, we find even *more* hidden depth (Excuse the pun!) of meaning that underscores God's preeminence over his creation. As we saw in the previous excerpt from the Babylonian creation account, the name given to the deified saltwater is Tiamat. In Genesis 1:2, the situation at the beginning of God's creative activity is described as "darkness . . . over the surface of the deep, and the Spirit of God . . . hovering over the waters." The word for "deep" in Hebrew is *təhôm* (תְּהוֹם)—a word linguistically related to Tiamat. But there is a huge difference in how this word is used in the biblical account! In the Babylonian creation epic, the deep is deified and somehow engenders the other gods. In the Bible the deep is merely one of the creations of the almighty, eternally existing God, put in place and controlled by him:

> He set the earth on its foundations;
>> it can never be moved.
> You covered it with the watery depths [təhôm] as
>> with a garment. (Ps 104:5–6)

In the biblical cosmogony, God doesn't arise out of these waters; his life-giving Spirit "hovers over them." We are again reminded even *by the way the biblical account is written* that God is above and beyond creation, not a part of it, however exalted or fearsome that part may be thought to be.

Already in the very first, seemingly ordinary, verse of the Bible, our understanding deepens by considering the creation accounts of Israel's ancient Near Eastern neighbors. The biblical author was no doubt aware of these accounts and, under the direction of the Spirit of God, communicated by his own artfully constructed account how radically different was the truth regarding Israel's God from the mythology of their neighbors. It is a fitting beginning for the biblical revelation to follow. Since the book of Genesis informs us that God created all that is, including human beings, he has the exclusive right and understanding to inform those human beings how they should live in relationship to him. His gracious desire for his human creations to realize their maximum possible life potential in relationship with him ultimately finds its fullest realization in Jesus Christ, who came "that they may have life, and have it to the full" (John 10:10). Through Jesus, the sovereign creator of heaven and earth once again creates new life (2 Cor 5:17).

THINGS TO CONSIDER

1. Would your confidence in God be the same if he were also a part of the created realm? Is eternal life for human beings possible apart from an eternal God? Why or why not? What would human beings lose if God were a created, evolved, or evolving being?

2. Do you have any problem with the fact that Genesis 1:2 seems to be alluding to a creature from Babylonian mythology (Tiamat/*təhôm*)? When the biblical author (or anyone else) refers to such a mythological creature, does that necessarily imply their belief in its actual existence?

3. Reflect on how God's creative activity in regeneration echoes his creative activity at the beginning of the Bible. How do the words that begin the Gospel of John reinforce this parallel?

2

— o —

MADE FOR
EACH OTHER

"I will make a helper suitable for him."
—GENESIS 2:18

D etails are important. Life and leadership blogger Don
McMinn provides a tragic example to illustrate this point:

The Space Shuttle Challenger disaster occurred when it broke
apart 73 seconds into its flight, leading to the deaths of seven
crew members. Disintegration began after an O-ring seal in
its right solid rocket booster failed at liftoff. . . . Why did the
O-ring fail? The morning of the launch, the temperature was
unusually cold and the rubber O-ring became brittle. NASA
scientists overlooked (or underestimated) the importance of
that one small detail, and the result was catastrophic.[1]

When we come to the Bible's extended account of the creation of human beings (Gen 2:4–25), we will see how "one small detail" regarding the female of the species can help us answer questions about this person God created for the man and how they should relate to each other. Ignoring this detail could have consequences equally disastrous as the *Challenger* catastrophe because even though we're in only the second chapter of the Bible, we're already encountering questions that strike at the very heart of the most intimate of human relationships. We need to pause our investigation here, however, and acknowledge that while there is great potential to discover deeper meaning as we explore this subject, there is also great potential for conflict. Human relationships, especially those between men and women, are delicate and dangerous conversation topics. Because of the tremendous potential for misunderstanding and controversy that can trigger relational IEDs along our path, we need to advance slowly and carefully as we dig up the treasures that await us here.

The verse we'll be focusing on (2:18) lies near the end of the creation story in the opening chapters of Genesis. By this point, God has created Adam and placed him in the garden. Nevertheless, the account goes on to reveal that God's work on his human creation had not yet reached its intended conclusion. God had made the male human in such a way that it was not good for him to be the sole representative of his species. Only after the completion of a second step would God's creative process involving humanity be fully realized. That second step in the process entailed creating "a helper suitable for [Adam]." We're told that such a helper was not to be found among the other species of animate creation already on the scene. No, the suitable helper would be something different that God would yet fashion. The helper would have to be just as distinct from the rest of creation as Adam was in order to be "suitable" for him. The deeper significance of such an important being lies somewhat hidden behind the English words used to describe this person.

Anyone who has learned a second language realizes that translating a word or expression from one language into another is often difficult. Frequently, it is impossible to translate word-for-word and accurately communicate the meaning the author intended. For example, consider the French expression *pomme de terre*. If we woodenly translate that phrase into English, we get "apple of earth." But the French expression has nothing at all to do with apples. It simply means "potato." And if the translation of words describing physical objects is sometimes not as straightforward as one might hope or expect, the situation is even more challenging when dealing with words describing something less concrete, such as a concept or category. This is certainly the case for the verse we're considering in this chapter.

The difficulty in capturing the intended meaning of the Hebrew words the NIV translates as "a helper suitable" is evidenced by the variety of expressions other English translations use to do so:

CEV: a suitable partner
ESV: a helper fit
HCSB: a helper as his complement
KJV: an help meet
NET: a companion . . . who corresponds
NLT: a helper who is just right

It is not merely to satisfy our curiosity that we need to clarify the meaning of this obscure phrase; our understanding of the created purpose of one-half of the human race hangs on it! Moreover, differences over the interpretation of this little phrase have sadly resulted in significant divisions in the church that continue today. Let's see what progress can be made toward shining some light on the source of so much conflict.

The Hebrew expression translated (in the NIV) as "helper suitable" (Gen 2:18) or "suitable helper" (Gen 2:20) consists of two terms: עֵזֶר כְּנֶגְדּוֹ ('ēzer kənegdô). The first term, עֵזֶר ('ēzer), has a general meaning of "help," "assistance," or "support."[2] One might suppose, therefore, that the word implies that the person this term describes would have a secondary or subordinate status (i.e., a "supporting" role). But a survey of the use of this word elsewhere in Scripture reveals that this is not the case. In the nineteen other occurrences of this common noun, almost all (sixteen) refer to the LORD's gracious activity on behalf of his people (Exod 18:4; Deut 33:7, 26, 29; Hos 13:9; Pss 20:2[3]; 33:20; 70:5[6]; 89:19[20]; 115:9, 10, 11; 121:1, 2; 124:8; 146:5). Perhaps the clearest of these examples is Psalm 121:1–2:

> I lift up my eyes to the mountains—
> where does my help ['ēzer] come from?
> My help ['ēzer] comes from the LORD,
> the Maker of heaven and earth.

One would not, hopefully, regard the Lord as secondary or subordinate to human beings!

The remaining three occurrences of the word (Isa 30:5; Ezek 12:14; Dan 11:34) all refer to someone seeking help or assistance from others in situations beyond their ability to handle. Surely at such critical times it is not likely that the beleaguered individual would seek the beneficent intervention of a person they deemed inferior or subordinate. If the individual could not effect their own deliverance from the situation, it is unlikely someone inferior would be able to accomplish the task. I don't reach for a smaller hammer when my large one won't drive the nail.

The second Hebrew term (*kanegdô*) is translated as "suitable" and consists of three parts: (1) a preposition meaning "like," "as," or "according to"; (2) a noun meaning "something or someone that is in front of or corresponding to something else"; and (3) a pronoun suffix meaning "his." The combination of these three grammatical components in this context roughly translates to "according to his correspondence." This unnatural English suggests someone God would fashion for the man who would correspond to him. Unlike the livestock, the birds in the sky, and all the wild animals God brings to the man (Gen 2:20), this new divine creation would correspond to the man in some way while also remaining distinct from him. She would be uniquely his counterpart and therefore uniquely suited for him. The Hebrew terms taken together, therefore, express the idea of someone who would correspond to the man in a way that nothing else could, enabling her to do for him those things beyond his own ability. Because nothing else in all creation can be described in this way, she is, from within that creation, the only "suitable helper" for him.

We must remember, however, that this uniquely suitable helper for the man is described in this way before the fall of humankind takes place. The entry of sin into God's good creation brought a radical pollution and brokenness to every part of it, including the creational relationship between the man and the woman, especially evident in the marriage relationship. This brokenness has unfortunately often resulted in the relegation of the woman's role in marriage to an inferior status—something that is foreign to the meaning of "suitable helper" (*ʿēzer kǝnegdô*) in Genesis 2:18.

The deeper meaning we've discovered in this important phrase ("suitable helper") should remind us that males and females are equally valued in God's kingdom; they are two sides of the same human coin. In the kingdom of God, gender is no more a ticket to preferential treatment than is ethnicity or socioeconomic status. As the apostle Paul put it, "In Christ Jesus you are all children of God through faith, for all of you who were baptized into Christ have clothed yourselves with Christ. There is neither Jew nor Gentile, neither slave nor free, nor is there male and female, for you are all one in Christ Jesus" (Gal 3:26–28). It is the responsibility of the church to present to the unbelieving world a picture of this new humanity God is creating and making available to all through faith in Jesus Christ. So believers should lead the way in showing the world what this kind of mutual respect and service between a man and a woman should look like both within and outside the marriage relationship.

What should be true for male-female relationships in general in the kingdom of God should be especially evident within the marriage relationship. Husbands should love and serve their wives just as their wives should love and serve them (1 Pet 3:1–7). This love between a husband and wife should epitomize human love and begin to reveal to unbelievers something of God's love for them. Because just as the woman is the only suitable helper for the man, God is the only suitable helper for humankind.

13

So let us turn to him for that help. In the words of the author of Hebrews, "Let us then approach God's throne of grace with confidence, so that we may receive mercy and find grace to help us in our time of need" (Heb 4:16).

THINGS TO CONSIDER

1. What has been your understanding of the role of women with respect to men and the role of men with respect to women in society, in the church, in the home? Has this brief investigation into the meaning of ʿēzer kənegdô modified your view?

2. How does your understanding of the created role of a person of the opposite gender affect the way you interact with that person? How could that interaction be modified to more accurately reflect what you have learned about the meaning of ʿēzer kənegdô?

3. Do you think the divinely created role of a woman with respect to a man or of a man with respect to a woman can be fulfilled only within a marriage relationship? If not, what are some ways these divinely created roles of men and women can be fulfilled in the broader society outside the marriage relationship?

3

—o—

AN EYE-OPENING
EXPERIENCE

She . . . sat down at the entrance ιυ Enaim.
—GENESIS 38:14

A "double entendre" is defined as "a word or phrase having a double sense."[1] Authors use it to take advantage of the multiple meanings words have in a language. By playing on those meanings, they can communicate at multiple levels at the same time and so deliver rhetorical power, depth, and pleasure to their readers. Who would not crack a smile, for example, at an author suggesting that through the skillful efforts of the detective the arsonist has met his match? Or be pleased with the appropriateness of a motorist miraculously escaping unscathed after totaling his car in Providence, Rhode Island? Unfortunately, however, because the multiple meanings of words in any one language are usually not able to be translated easily into another language, the double entendres that appear in the Hebrew Old Testament often go unobserved and unappreciated. This is the case for Genesis 38:14. This seemingly ordinary verse contains a Hebrew wordplay, a double entendre, that has become lost in its translation into English. Unearthing this wordplay will reveal a surprising and powerful significance we have probably overlooked.

But before we begin digging up this buried meaning, we need to survey the surrounding literary landscape. When we do so, we find that we're near the beginning of a long story that extends from Genesis 37 to the very end of the book. It is the story about Joseph and his brothers. Although most outlines and summaries of this extended account focus on Joseph, the actual, though seemingly unlikely, star of the narrative is one of his brothers, Judah. It is Judah who undergoes a radical metamorphosis over the course of these chapters from resentful brother and callous son to self-sacrificial leader. Genesis 38:14 foreshadows this change at the very beginning of the story, though in a way that is unfortunately hidden to those unfamiliar with Hebrew.

Admittedly, at the beginning of "the Joseph story" (Gen 37–50), Judah does not appear very praiseworthy at all. Like the rest of his brothers, Judah resents Joseph because of his father's special treatment of this young upstart. Jacob had made a special robe for his favored son that daily displayed to his brothers his special family status. Joseph surely doesn't help matters much with his naivete. He only adds fuel to the fires of resentment by recounting to his brothers dreams in which they bow down to him (37:5–9). And he rubs salt in the wound by tattling on his brothers to his father (37:2). But these unwise behaviors hardly justify what his brothers do next. When they get Joseph alone in the field, away from the protective presence of their father, they tear off his special tunic and throw him into a cistern while they decide what else to do with him. At this point, Judah steps forward to lead his brothers in carrying out the terrible plan he had devised (37:26–27). Judah proposes that they sell Joseph as a slave to passing merchants heading down to Egypt. Then they would stain his tunic with blood, shove it in their father's face when they returned home, and allow him to (incorrectly, of course) conclude that a wild animal had torn his favorite son to pieces (37:26–28, 31–33). It is hard to imagine the heartlessness of Judah as he stood by and watched his father's misery over the loss of his son. Judah could have ended Jacob's devastating anguish with just a few words, but he chose not to speak them.

Such is the picture of the ancestor of the Messiah with which we're confronted in Genesis 37. He is hardly the upright character we might have expected an esteemed patriarch of the Hebrews to be. This faulty human being is the central character in the side drama that plays out in the very next chapter. And things don't start out any better. We're told at the beginning of chapter 38 that Judah had left his own people and married a Canaanite woman. Surely Judah had been told how his great-grandfather Abraham had made his servant swear that he wouldn't get a wife for his son Isaac "from the daughters of the Canaanites" (24:3). But Judah chose to leave the company of the people of God and dwell instead among the Canaanites, ignoring the warnings from history preserved in the account of Lot and Sodom (ch. 19). Not only did Judah dwell among the Canaanites, but he married one and had three children by her. But here is where the plot twists.

Judah's first son married a woman named Tamar. Then Judah's first son died, leaving Tamar a childless widow. In keeping with the custom at the time, Judah gave Tamar to his second son as a wife so that through him she could have offspring to carry on the name of her deceased first husband. But this second son also died, leaving Tamar without a child. Judah had one son left, but he was understandably reluctant to give him to this apparent black widow who seemed to bury husbands almost as fast as she acquired them. Tamar then stepped forward to take matters into her own hands.

By custom, she had a right to Judah's third son, but Judah had been denying her that right. So after Judah's own wife died, Tamar decided to procure a son for her deceased husband from Judah himself. She dressed up as a prostitute and positioned herself along the route she knew Judah would be traveling. She caught Judah's eye, and he, not knowing who she was, had sexual relations with her. As promise of future payment for the experience, he gave her his staff, his seal, and its cord. Tamar returned to her normal life and in the course of time began evidencing that she was pregnant. Thinking she was guilty of having illicit sex, Judah decreed that she should be burned to death. Tamar then showed him his staff, seal, and cord, and Judah realized what had happened. Acknowledging that she had done no more than what she was entitled to by custom, Judah confessed that she had done what was right for her deceased husband and he had not. Judah allowed her to live, and she gave birth to twins, one of whom became the ancestor of Jesus himself (Perez, see Matt 1:3).

Chapter 38 presents us with this interesting little soap opera, but what does it have to do with our seemingly ordinary verse? The fact that the connection is not obvious explains why the deeper significance of our verse has remained hidden for so long.

Before we uncover its relevance, we need to consider one other piece of information: the change in Judah over the course of the Joseph story—and that change is remarkable!

After a series of events that underscore God's providential care and sovereign control of history, Joseph found himself the number-two man in Egypt, dispensing grain during an extensive famine. When Joseph's brothers came to Egypt to get grain for their own households, they ended up standing before Joseph himself. It had been so long and Joseph appeared so different that his brothers didn't even recognize him, although he recognized them. (For more details regarding this key word "recognize," see the next chapter.) Joseph put them through a series of tests that made it clear that Benjamin, the only other son of his mother Rachel, had become his father's new favorite, just as Joseph had been earlier. By framing Benjamin for a crime he did not commit, Joseph put his brothers in a position to get rid of this new favorite son just as they got rid of him so many years before. Once again Judah took the lead among his brothers, but this time his words revealed that he was a changed man.

Many years previously, in chapter 37, Judah's resentment over his father's favoritism for Joseph led Judah to concoct a plan to get rid of him. But in chapter 44, Judah does not speak in favor of getting rid of Benjamin, this new favorite son who has taken the place of Joseph in his father's affections. No, Judah does something else entirely. Judah offers himself as a slave to Joseph so that his brother Benjamin can return to his father. What a reversal! Judah knows he is not loved as much as Benjamin. But instead of resentment, he offers himself in place of Benjamin so that his father and this son who is loved more than any of his brothers can be reunited. Somewhere along the line Judah had a radical transformation of character that has resulted in this selfless act. We must return to chapter 38 to find out where this change began.

It is in chapter 38 that Judah says about Tamar, "She is more righteous than I" (38:26). This verse could also be translated "She is right, not I."[2] This confession reveals that Judah has become aware that he was on the wrong track. He acknowledges his error and begins to change. That change blossoms into self-sacrifice near the end of the Joseph story. But it begins right here after a self-realization brought about by a crafty daughter-in-law. And now the hidden, deeper significance of the double entendre in our verse is ready to be unveiled.

Tamar perpetrated her deception of Judah at a place called "the entrance to Enaim" (38:14). The Hebrew word translated here as "entrance" is *petah*, which can also mean "opening."[3] Also, in Hebrew the names of people and places are selected not only because they sound nice, they also actually *mean* something. The name of the town mentioned here, Enaim, means "springs" or "eyes."[4] It was probably a place identified by the presence of springs. That the word for springs (watery circles on the ground) can also be used to denote eyes (watery circles on the face) is understandable. So when the alternative meanings of these two Hebrew words are considered, we discover the surprising significance the narrator has skillfully woven into this story to reveal the point where Judah comes to his transformative self-realization. It occurs "at the entrance to Enaim" or "the opening of the eyes." Judah's eyes are opened to his own need for change at a place that can be translated as "the opening of the eyes"!

Once Judah's eyes were opened, he acknowledged Tamar's right to do what she did and also his own failure to provide for the continuation of his deceased son's family line. Tamar risked her life to continue the life (family line) of her deceased husband, just as Judah would later risk his life to continue the life of Benjamin. Because of what Tamar did, Perez and his brother were born. Perez became the ancestor of David and the Messiah. One righteous act profoundly affected the life of Judah, a key figure in the history of Israel, and was used by God in his plan of redemption that would culminate in the work of Jesus Christ.

THINGS TO CONSIDER

1. God used Tamar to bring Judah to a realization that he was on the wrong track. Who has God used in your life to open your eyes to the emptiness of life apart from God? How could God use you to open someone else's eyes?

2. Does it make you feel uncomfortable that God used Tamar's sexual deception of her father-in-law as part of his redemptive plan to bring the Messiah into the world? Is God limited in the means he may use to accomplish his purposes? Are we? Is there a difference between God's moral compass and ours?

3. Tamar risked her life to provide life for her deceased husband. Judah offered his life to preserve the life of Benjamin. Jesus gave his life for us. Is there anything you would be willing to offer your life for? What are you currently giving your life to?

4

—o—

Recognizing
"Recognize"

"See if you recognize . . ." Judah recognized . . .
—Genesis 38:25-26

I n the previous chapter, we saw how the final section of the
book of Genesis, though commonly referred to as the Joseph
story, is more accurately described as a story about the remarkable
transformation of Joseph's brother, Judah, the ancestor of Jesus
Christ. In this chapter, we'll see that this extraordinary and radical
change in Judah is signaled by three key passages that are stitched
together in Hebrew by a thread that is difficult to see in English
translations but that adds a surprising depth of meaning to this
wonderfully recounted narrative. That thread is the Hebrew word
usually translated "recognize" (from the root נכר *n-k-r*), which is
found only in these three passages in this entire story.

The first of these three passages presents to us a portrait of Judah in his unreformed state, with all his warts and blemishes. Judah is the one who hatched the plan to get rid of Joseph, the one their father infuriatingly favored. Judah figured he could remove Joseph from the picture and make a profit at the same time by selling him to Ishmaelite traders for twenty shekels of silver (Gen 37:26–28). Because of the profound change in Judah's character over the course of the rest of this narrative, and to help us fully appreciate the magnitude of that change, it is necessary for us to dwell a bit longer on his initial character failings.

To be fair to Judah, we can understand his resentment over Joseph, even if we don't necessarily approve of it. No doubt Judah believed that he, and not Joseph, should be the one receiving the special attention of their father, Jacob. After all, by tradition and custom, it was his right. All his older brothers had previously disqualified themselves by their behavior. Reuben, Jacob's firstborn son, had forfeited his rights to primacy among his brothers by brazenly sleeping with his father's concubine (35:22; 49:3–4). The next sons in the line of inheritance rights were Simeon and Levi. But these two also fell out of favor with their father Jacob because of their overzealous reaction to the violation of their sister Dinah by Shechem (34:30; 49:5–7). That meant Judah, the fourth in line, should have been granted the rights and privileges of the firstborn. Instead, he had to contend with not just another brother but with the *next-to-youngest* brother receiving his father's favor instead of him. And Joseph's arrogance and fraternal insensitivity did nothing to ameliorate the situation but only rubbed salt in an already painful wound.

The simmering resentment and jealousy of the brothers, felt

most keenly by Judah, their leader, eventually boiled over into violence and subsequent deception. They rid themselves of the hated Joseph by selling him off to passing caravanners as a slave and concocting a plan to fool their father about what they had done. They dipped Joseph's robe in the blood of a goat to make it look like he'd been killed by a wild animal, and then they brought the robe to their father. At this point in the story, we need to slow way down and give careful attention to the specific words the narrator uses, because here is where the thin thread that ties together the subplot of Judah's transformation makes its first appearance. When Jacob was presented with Joseph's blood-stained robe, presumably by Judah, who was leading the brothers in this deception, he was told to "examine it" to see whether it was, in fact, Joseph's robe (37:32). The hidden significance of this exhortation is more easily seen when the underlying Hebrew is observed: הַכֶּר־נָא *hakker-nāʾ* (from the root נכר *n-k-r*). That the narrator wants readers and hearers to take notice of this key Hebrew root is evident by its immediate reappearance in the following verse (37:33): "He [Jacob] recognized it [וַיַּכִּירָהּ *wayyakkîrāh* from the root נכר *n-k-r*] and said, 'It is my son's robe!'" What we as readers *recognize* about Judah at this point in the story is his utter callousness as he stood there watching his father's emotional collapse as he *recognized* the bloody robe of his cherished son and assumed the worst. Judah was willing to let his father's thoughts descend into the most gruesome possibilities without saying one word to alleviate his anguish. This first use of the word "recognize" marks the low point of Judah's character in the story. On the road of his moral transformation, Judah has a long, long way to go.

The second of the three passages that use this Hebrew word to signal important points in Judah's transformation is found in the very next chapter, Genesis 38. We pick up the story with Judah having been deceived by his daughter-in-law Tamar into providing offspring to perpetuate her deceased husband's family line. That her late husband's family should have taken steps to keep her husband's name alive was her legitimate expectation. But after two of Judah's sons had been married to Tamar and died, he was unwilling to risk a third. Not willing to leave this issue unaddressed, Tamar decided to take matters into her own hands. Pretending to be a prostitute, Tamar tricked an unwitting Judah into impregnating her and leaving with her his staff and seal with its cord as promise of his future payment. After some time, Tamar's pregnancy became obvious and was reported to Judah. Not knowing that he was the father of the unborn child and believing she had become pregnant through prostitution, Judah directed that Tamar be burned to death. But at that critical moment Tamar revealed Judah's paternity by returning to him his staff and seal with its cord that he had left with her when he slept with her. Readers and hearers of the Hebrew narrative at this point would not miss the narrator's intentional connection of the deception of Judah with Judah's previous deception of Jacob. Because when Tamar directs Judah to "see if you recognize whose seal and cord and staff these are" (38:25), she uses *exactly the same Hebrew construction* Judah had used when he deceived his father: הַכֶּר־נָא *hakker-nā* (from the root נכר *n-k-r*). Once again, to make sure no one could miss the verbal thread that sews these two events together, the narrator repeats the Hebrew root in the very next verse: "Judah recognized [וַיַּכֵּר *wayyakkēr* from the root נכר‎ n-k-r] them" (38:26). As we saw in the previous chapter, this is the point in Judah's life where his eyes are opened to his unrighteousness and the transformation of his character becomes a real possibility.

The third passage stitched together with the previous two by the Hebrew thread נכר‎ n-k-r occurs in chapter 42, near the end of the narrative of Judah's transformation. It had been over twenty years since Judah and his brothers had sold Joseph to the caravanners headed to Egypt.[1] In the brothers' minds, the probability was very high that Joseph was no longer alive. If he had somehow managed to stay alive all this time, he would have been a slave longer than he had been free. So the likelihood that his brothers would encounter him in their dealings with the governor of Egypt was infinitesimally small. But that is exactly what happened. With unmistakably providential acts, God had accomplished what was seemingly impossible: Pharaoh had placed Joseph in charge of administering the entire land of Egypt. And it was to this royal administrator that Joseph's brothers were directed when they came to Egypt to buy grain to provide for themselves and their families through the protracted famine that was devastating the entire region. But, of course, Joseph's brothers were oblivious to the fact that they were standing in the presence of their own brother. Their certainty that he was now dead, the passage of over two decades, and his foreign language and appearance rendered him unrecognizable to them. In this unlikely meeting between Joseph and his brothers, the narrator reminds us of the previous two stages of Judah's transformation by again using the word "recognize" (three[2] times in only two verses) to mark the culmination of Judah's transformation:

- **42:7:** "As soon as Joseph saw his brothers,
  he *recognized* them"
  (וַיַּכִּרֵם *wayyakkīrēm* from the root נכר)
- **42:8:** "Joseph *recognized* his brothers"
  (וַיַּכֵּר *wayyakēr* from the root נכר)
- **42:8:** "but they didn't *recognize* him"
  (הִכִּרֻהוּ *hikkīrūhû* from the root נכר)

Joseph had indeed changed, but so had his brothers—especially Judah, whom the narrator has marked for special attention through his use of the root נכר. Joseph thought he recognized his brothers, but he couldn't see their inner transformation. That transformation comes to light only when they have the opportunity to get rid of their father's new favorite son, Benjamin, without any blame accruing to themselves. But instead of leaving Benjamin behind in Egypt as a slave, they cast their lot with his and return to face the judgment of the Egyptian governor (44:10, 13). Judah's amazing transformation then becomes clear to Joseph when Judah offers himself to be a slave instead of Benjamin (44:33). At last Joseph can see the true Judah he only thought he recognized before. At this point, Joseph reveals himself to his brothers so that they can recognize him as well (45:3).

By his skillful literary use of the Hebrew root נכר *n-k-r* at three important points in his recounting of this story, the narrator has revealed crucial stages in Judah's transformation. Judah has gone from (1) a self-centered and bitter rival of a favored son to (2) a person who recognizes the ugly truth about himself to (3) one who is ready to sacrifice himself for another—even one who has been arguably unjustly favored over him. This account of Judah's amazing transformation contributes to the larger theme of the book of Genesis, which reveals how God separates out one person (Abraham) through whom he would bless all nations.[3] That divine intent involves guiding and protecting that chosen line from both external *and* internal threats until it finds its ultimate fulfillment in Jesus Christ. In the Joseph story, we see God goading Judah, the ancestor of the Messiah, back onto the correct path by putting him in situations where he could recognize important truths about himself and others.

Through faith in Jesus Christ, believers have become adopted members of the family line of Abraham (Rom 4:16–17). Like Judah, we have had our eyes opened to our unrighteousness. Like Judah was molded from a self-centered person into someone willing to sacrifice himself for Benjamin, we are being conformed to the likeness of the One who sacrificed himself for others. And like Judah, when we stray from the path of life, we shouldn't be surprised when God goads us back onto the right path, helping us to recognize once again truth about him and about ourselves.

THINGS TO CONSIDER

1. God coordinated the confluence of the shrewdness of Tamar and the moral laxity of Judah to lead to Judah's self-realization and the beginning of his transformation. How might God be working in the circumstances of your own life to cause you to recognize the truth about yourself?

2. Judah recognized Joseph as "the man who is lord over the land" (Gen 42:30, 33) but not as his brother. Joseph recognized Judah as his brother but didn't recognize his transformed character. When Jesus came into the world, "the world did not recognize him" (John 1:10). Have you recognized Jesus for who he truly is? How could your recognition improve?

3. When God led Judah to recognize the truth about himself, his character changed dramatically. He became willing to sacrifice himself for another person—even someone who, by the world's standards, was unjustly favored above him. Since God has led you to recognize the truth about yourself, how has this changed how you value others?

5

— ◦ —

In Your
Dreams

*Pharaoh told them his dreams, but no
one could interpret them for him.*
—Genesis 41:8

At first glance, there appears to be nothing surprising about
Genesis 41:8. It seems to simply recount that Pharaoh, like
many of us at times, has had a strange dream or two whose significance was beyond his understanding. Those of us who have
the occasional strange dream enjoy recounting it to others but
after doing so usually laugh it off and forget about it. We regard
it as inconsequential and perhaps simply the result of something
as mundane as a spicy late-night snack. It is nothing we take
seriously. But if we look more closely at the original language in

which Pharaoh's dream is recounted, we find that it communicates so much more than we could have imagined.

The smooth English translation of Genesis 41:8 hides a significant textual problem in the underlying Hebrew that highlights the central question being communicated by this context: Who is wiser? Is it "all the magicians and wise men of Egypt"? Or is it Joseph—the lone, imprisoned worshiper of the true God? The Hebrew of the second sentence of this verse reveals a single, important difference from the smoother English translation. That difference can be seen when a more formal translation of the Hebrew is compared with the NIV (with italics added to highlight the difference):

> My formal translation: "Pharaoh told them his *dream*,
>   but no one could interpret them for him."
> The NIV translation: "Pharaoh told them his *dreams*,
>   but no one could interpret them for him."

Instead of translating the singular noun in the Hebrew text as "dream," most translations (such as the NIV), because of the disagreement in grammatical number between the singular "dream" and the plural "them" later in the sentence, assume (incorrectly, we will see) that an error has crept into the text, and so they translate the singular Hebrew noun as a plural: "dreams." The difference from the English translation amounts to only one letter: "dream" versus "dreams." And one might think that simply adding one letter for the sake of smoother English is not such a big deal. But in this case, it certainly *is* a big deal. As we will see, that one letter has extraordinary significance!

Unlike the official wise men, Joseph is able to explain that Pharaoh's two dream episodes "are one and the same" (41:25); that is, they are describing the same event. Pharaoh didn't have *two* dreams; he had one dream that came to him in two parts. This understanding is something that was beyond the perception of Egypt's most respected brain trust and proved beyond any doubt in Pharaoh's mind that God's sole representative was far more "discerning and wise" than anyone else in Egypt, including Pharaoh himself (41:39). Consequently, Pharaoh deemed Joseph worthy of having all Egyptians submit to his orders (41:40).

But wait, there's more! The biblical narrator of this account leads readers of the original language into the realization that Joseph's conclusion is correct by means of another, extraordinary literary technique that involves the elaborate use of something as ordinary as adjectives. Through his exceedingly careful selection of the adjectives that he uses to describe the cows and the grain in Pharaoh's dreams, the narrator *implicitly* communicates to the observant Hebrew reader the same fact that Joseph later *explicitly* communicates to Pharaoh: the two parts of the dream are communicating the same message.

Pharaoh's two-part dream is recounted no fewer than three times by three different people, and the differences between their accounts are laden with significance. The narrator himself provides the first account of the dream. Out of the many adjectives he uses to describe the good and bad cows and the good and bad grain, the narrator has taken pains to use only one adjective that is the same. This is his clue to observant readers that these two dream episodes are related:

THE NARRATOR'S ACCOUNT OF PHARAOH'S
TWO-PART DREAM (41:1–7)

GOOD COWS	GOOD GRAIN	BAD COWS	BAD GRAIN
יפות מראה	בריאות	רעות מראה	דקות
בריאת בשר	טבות	דקות בשר	שדופת קדים
יפת המראה	הבריאות	רעות המראה	דקות
הבריאת	מלאות	דקת הבשר	

Notice that the narrator's description of the good cows and the good grain share the adjective בריאת, in black type (its alternative spelling is בריאות). The bad cows and the bad grain share the adjective דקת, in black boxes (its alternative spelling is דקות). By using only a single adjective to describe both good cows and grain and another one to describe both bad cows and grain, the narrator hasn't given everything away all at once. He has provided just enough clues for readers to conclude that these dream episodes seem to have something to do with each other.

But these clues are missed by the hapless Pharaoh. He is not only oblivious to the meaning of his two-part dream, he is not even able to recognize that it *is* a two-part dream. The narrator has ingeniously communicated Pharaoh's obliviousness by carefully ensuring that in Pharaoh's recounting of his dream experience *not a single adjective* used to describe the cows and grain is the same:

PHARAOH'S ACCOUNT OF HIS TWO-PART
DREAM (41:17–24)

GOOD COWS	GOOD GRAIN	BAD COWS	BAD GRAIN
בריאות בשר	מלאת	דלות	צנמות
יפת תאר	טבות	רעות תאר מאד	דקות
בריאת	טבות	רקות בשר	שדפות קדים
		רקות	דקת
		רעות	

If you carefully compare the Hebrew adjectives used to describe the good cows and the good grain, and the bad cows and the bad grain, you can see that there is not a single one in common. One has to concede that this is quite a feat of literary skill considering how many adjectives have been used! This level of disagreement between so many adjectives can certainly not be coincidental. This is the narrator's way of communicating Pharaoh's cluelessness—a cluelessness shared by Pharaoh's magicians and wise men.

In contrast to the lack of wisdom on the part of the wise men and Pharaoh, Joseph immediately recognizes both the connectedness and meaning of what he hears. And the narrator has communicated this by the close correspondence between adjectives in Joseph's explanation of Pharaoh's experience:

JOSEPH'S ACCOUNT OF PHARAOH'S TWO-PART DREAM (41:25–27)

GOOD COWS	GOOD GRAIN	BAD COWS	BAD GRAIN
טבת	טבת	רקות	רקות
		רעת	שדפות הקדים

In Joseph's account, the good cows and good grain are both טבת; the bad cows and the bad grain are both רקות. The specific adjectives used underscore Joseph's assertion that "the dreams [Hebrew: dream] of Pharaoh are one and the same" (41:25).

The extraordinary level of care taken by the narrator to communicate this contest between God's representative and Egypt's representatives extends all the way down to the level of adjectives. At the beginning of the contest, there was nothing about God's representative that suggested he would end up victorious. He was an imprisoned foreigner standing alone against an august assemblage of Egypt's most highly regarded intellectuals. But Joseph worshiped the one true God and not the false gods venerated by the Egyptians. And, as Joseph had earlier explained to Pharaoh's cupbearer and baker (40:8) and now to Pharaoh himself (41:16), interpretations belong to that one true God. It is not the number or status of those who worship a god that establishes anything about that god. It is rather the attributes of the god who is worshiped that determine that god's praiseworthiness. And there is only one all-knowing and all-powerful God. As he had for Israel in the past, God now makes clear to Egypt that he is the one who controls the events of history, and so it is his direction that must be followed if deliverance is to be realized. Those who heed that direction will ultimately be proven correct and rewarded.

At the beginning of Genesis 41, Joseph was in a foreign prison. Humanly speaking, his situation was hopeless. Yet by the end of the chapter, Joseph has been placed over the entire land of Egypt, second only to Pharaoh, riding in a chariot and wearing the accoutrements of royalty. History is indeed in God's hands because he is its author, orchestrator, and the one who brings it to the culmination he has ordained. This truth becomes so clear that even Pharaoh has to acknowledge it (41:39).

God's hand in historical events is not always easy to see or believe. One can only imagine the near despair Joseph felt as his situation went from bad to worse. He was betrayed by his family, dragged off to a country whose language and culture were foreign to him, put on the auction block and sold as a slave, framed for a serious crime, and left without reason for hope. But all these things, it turns out, were necessary for him to achieve God's gracious deliverance. As Joseph later says to his brothers (no doubt after lengthy retrospection): "You intended to harm me, but God intended it for good to accomplish what is now being done, the saving of many lives" (50:20).

In the same way, God's purposes through Jesus were not immediately apparent. He was maligned, marginalized, and eventually tortured and crucified. It must have been difficult for people to believe that God was behind the events that led to such an ignominious end. But Joseph's words to his brothers could have been spoken by Jesus himself to his persecutors: "You intended to harm me, but God intended it for good to accomplish what is now being done, the saving of many lives" (50:20).

The God who knows the difference between one dream and two is the same God who controls the events of history to accomplish his appointed gracious ends. We can trust that he also uses the details of our lives in his grand purposes, even when every circumstance seems to be arguing to the contrary.

THINGS TO CONSIDER

1. God placed Joseph in a situation where he was called upon to present the truth, even though that truth could negatively impact his circumstances. His news of a coming famine could have resulted in extended prison time for him or even death. The temptation to limit his message to only good news was surely present. What would you do if you were placed in a similar situation? Have you already experienced a situation like that?

2. Joseph's circumstances for over two years had been miserable. It would be hard enough for an Egyptian in prison, but as a foreigner Joseph would have found his situation even more difficult. He surely questioned why God had allowed those things to happen to him. Only later did he realize how God had used his experiences to accomplish "the saving of many lives." Have you had experiences that you later recognized God had used to accomplish his purposes?

3. Joseph was called to deliver a message to Pharaoh and his officials that would preserve their lives during a coming

famine. But these were the very people whose justice system had resulted in his unjust imprisonment. How do you help those in an unjust system without contributing to the perpetuation of injustice?

6

—o—

IMAGE PROBLEMS

*"You shall not make for yourself an image in
the form of anything in heaven above or on
the earth beneath or in the waters below. You
shall not bow down to them or worship them."*
—EXODUS 20:4-5

Those who have spent any time in the church have no doubt heard the Ten Commandments recited, preached, or taught. Many of us have memorized them. They are even found (still) in some public schools, courts, and government buildings. So the idea that these familiar verses could have any deeper significance that would be surprising to us seems a bit of a stretch. And, if we're honest, we might admit to a bit of disinclination toward spending any time looking more closely at commandments, because, really, who likes commandments?

Most of us simply don't like being told what to do. We don't

like instructions, directions, commands, orders, rules, requirements, or laws. All those words seem too confining or restrictive,
like they have the potential to squeeze the life out of life. Perhaps
our aversion to commands is due to the fact that we're so used
to human commands and all the human problems that surface
both in giving them and receiving them. But divine commands
don't have these human problems or limitations, of course. They
come from entirely pure motives and have wonderful ends in
view. These divine commands are given in order to strengthen
our relationship with God and to lead us to fullness of life—the
deep, rich, satisfying lives God desires for us. In other words,
God's commandments don't keep out life, they describe what
true life is! So despite our possible negative initial reaction to the
word "command," it is worthwhile for us to give some further
attention here to one of these divine commandments. And when
we do, we'll find that it has a surprising, life-promoting significance we may have overlooked.

In the book of Exodus, God delivers the Ten Commandments
to his people, through Moses, at the very beginning of their
formation as a nation. They've come out of Egypt in spectac-
ular fashion and are gathered together at Mount Sinai, where
God delivers this revelation to them. These commandments
are something like Israel's national charter that should shape
their life as the unique people of God. God has Moses repeat
these same commandments to his people in the book of
Deuteronomy, right before they cross over into the promised
land. God does this to remind his people of the most important
things for them to remember. And right at the beginning of this
list of most important things are the first two commandments.
They are listed first because they are the most important of

the most important things. That's why we need to give them a closer look.

The first commandment in 20:3 ("You shall have no other gods before me") sparks some questions of its own. For example, who are the "other gods," and what is the nature of their being or existence, if any? And what does it mean to "have" these gods "before" the true God? Although answering these questions would certainly yield for us a deeper understanding of this familiar commandment, we will move on to consider what is usually numbered as the second commandment (which the Roman Catholic Church and the Lutheran Church combine with the previous commandment into one).[1] This second commandment is (coincidentally) the second-longest commandment,[2] surpassed only by the fourth, which pertains to keeping the Sabbath day holy. When we look more closely at two key words in the second commandment, we begin to realize something of the depth of the pool we've just dived into.

The commandment (Exod 20:4–5) forbids making an "image" (פֶּסֶל *pesel*) in the "form" (תְּמוּנָה *təmûnâ*) of anything in the entire creation. Artistic, right-brained people might be initially dismayed when hearing these words and conclude that this commandment is unfairly aimed at squelching their creative impulses. But one can arrive at that conclusion only if one stops reading before the sentence that immediately follows: "You shall not bow down to them or worship them." Clearly, then, what is being prohibited is making images *with the intention of worshiping them.*[3] Perhaps, we might think, even though making images of *false* gods to worship is unquestionably forbidden, it might not be forbidden to make images of the *true* God who is worthy of worship. Some argue, for example, that this is precisely what was happening in the incident involving the golden calf in Exodus 32. According to this view, Aaron fashioned the calf to be a visible representation of the true God for the Israelites to worship.[4] Indeed, in Egypt, where the Israelites had spent roughly four hundred years, "the sacred Apis and Mnevis bulls . . . were always regarded as being the 'living images' of divinities."[5] So it wouldn't be surprising if the Israelites (or at least Aaron) were attempting to do something similar by providing the calf as an image of the true God. And, we might be asking ourselves, what is so bad or dangerous about making an image to represent the true God who is worthy of worship? It is not an overstatement to say that the answer to that question strikes at the very heart of what it means to be a human being! To delve into this critically important issue more deeply, and to understand the connections this commandment has with later New Testament teaching, we need to explore two Greek roots: εικ- (eik-) and ὁμοιω- (homoiō-).

In the Septuagint (the Greek translation of the Old Testament), 20:4 uses the words εἰδωλον (eidōlon, from which we get our English word "idol") and ὁμοιωμα (homoiōma, translated as "form"). While there is little difficulty with the first word, the meaning of the second word raises questions. The root of this word (ὁμοιω- homoiō-) has surprising significance because it appears for the very first time in the Septuagint in Genesis 1:26, where we're told that humankind was made in the image of God, in his "likeness" (ὁμοιωσιν homoiōsin). This statement is applied to nothing else in creation and so sets human beings apart from all other creatures. But in what way human beings are made in the likeness of God is not entirely clear. Sometimes other words in the same context can help us understand the meaning of an unfamiliar word. However, to further complicate matters in this case, the word "likeness" is paired with the word "image" (εικονα *eikona*), another word whose precise meaning is unclear. Certainly, it can't refer to a physical form because God has no form (Deut 4:12). Most scholars understand bearing God's image and likeness to mean being "a faithful and adequate *representation*, though not a facsimile."[6] That is, human beings are created as God's representatives, not as his duplicates. Of course, we can represent him well only if we have a relationship with him. That is why some scholars go so far as to say that "humans are created in such a way that their very existence is intended to be their relationship to God."[7]

We're beginning to see the magnitude of the significance of the second commandment's prohibition. It addresses an issue that touches on our "very existence"! And this significance is further magnified by the way the two key Greek roots (εικ- [*eik-*] and ὁμοιω- [*homoiō-*]) that we found in Genesis 1:26 are used in two key New Testament passages. The first of these is Romans 1:21–23:

> Although they knew God, they neither glorified him as God nor gave thanks to him, but their thinking became futile and their foolish hearts were darkened. Although they claimed to be wise, they became fools and exchanged the glory of the immortal God for images [εικονος *eikonos*] made to look like [ὁμοιωματι *homoiōmati*] a mortal human being and birds and animals and reptiles.

These verses describe two radically different paths human beings can take. In one, they glorify God and give thanks to him (relational activities). In the other, they glorify and give thanks to images they have created (unrelational activities because the lifeless images cannot respond). The latter activity is described as "futile" and "foolish." We must conclude, then, that human beings are on the only legitimate path when they pursue a relationship with their Creator instead of futilely pursuing a relationship with something they themselves have created. That is, the true and only legitimate divine image-bearers can only find complete fulfillment in their relationship with the One whose image they bear, instead of in futile attempts to relegate that divine image-bearing to other things.

The second New Testament passage takes this idea even further. Romans 8:29 says, "Those God foreknew he also predestined to be conformed to the image [εικονος *eikonos*] of his Son, that he might be the firstborn among many brothers and sisters."

Conforming to God's image, then, seems to necessarily imply a relationship with God by means of our relationship with his Son, with whom believers are brothers and sisters. Note that believers are being conformed to the image of Jesus Christ, who has the closest possible relationship with the Father.

Through our examination of the Greek roots for the words "image" and "likeness," the enormous, life-promoting implications of the second commandment can now be much more clearly understood. God created us to be in a relationship with him. Although we may not be able to fully describe all the implications of our bearing God's image, this is at least one way we are like him. We are created to be relational beings like our relational Creator. We have the ability, unlike anything else in creation, to have a relationship with him. This is what it means for us to be truly human, to live into our created purpose. When we ignore the second commandment and choose instead to create images of *other* living things with which we futilely seek to have a relationship instead of with the true God, we deny our creational purpose as human beings. By doing so, it is not possible to find the fulfillment or true joy God intends for us.

We acknowledged at the beginning of this chapter that some of us may view the commandments as restrictive and as having the potential to squeeze the life out of life. The reality, however, is just the opposite. The second commandment (as all the commandments do) shows us where to find the fullest possible life. Indeed, Jesus said about his disciples, "I have come that they may have life, and have it to the full" (John 10:10). The fullest possible life means having the closest possible relationship with God. In other words, it means becoming more and more like Jesus.

THINGS TO CONSIDER

1. Many of us may have concluded that we're satisfying the second commandment by not making idols to worship. But the second commandment doesn't just tell us what we *should not* do, it also reminds us what we *should* be doing to experience life at its fullest, as God intended. How would you rate your progress toward this goal?

2. How do you think most unbelievers would describe a successful human being? Does the way you live your life show them that you think any differently? In what ways could unbelievers see that Christians value their relationship with God above everything else? If they can't see that we value our relationship with God by the way we live, does that mean Christians are guilty of violating the second commandment?

3. Bearing God's image well means nurturing our relationship with him. So what can believers do individually and corporately to deepen our relationship with God? What do we find the disciples and Jesus himself doing in the New Testament?

7

—o—

GRACE IN PLACE

"They must make restitution in full, add a fifth
of the value to it and give it all to the owner
on the day they present their guilt offering."
—LEVITICUS 6:5

The instructions that fill the book of Leviticus can be somewhat off-putting and tiresome for believers today who
may struggle to understand the relevance of these regulations
now that Christ has come. In fact, many of us might expect to
encounter in Leviticus the same level of mind-numbing verbiage
as we would in reviewing the picayune details in the bylaws of
our neighborhood homeowner's association. But there are good
reasons for us to give serious attention to the laws of Leviticus.
First, Christ fulfills these laws. As the apostle Paul put it, "Christ
is the culmination of the law" (Rom 10:4). Because all the biblical
laws and commandments (including those found in Leviticus)

find their fulfillment or ultimate realization in the life, death, and resurrection of Jesus, it stands to reason that we can better understand the life, death, and resurrection of Jesus only if we better understand the laws and commandments he fulfills. Second, an awareness of the nature and purpose of these regulations helps believers to grasp not only what Christ has accomplished for them but also to realize what sort of people they should be becoming. Once again, the apostle Paul clarifies the situation for us: "Those God foreknew he also predestined to be conformed to the image of his Son" (Rom 8:29). Since Christ fulfills the law, and believers are being conformed to Christ's image, exploring the nature and purpose of Old Testament laws can help believers realize how they can participate with the Holy Spirit in their intended transformation toward Christlikeness.

And such an exploration of Old Testament laws is not as burdensome as some might fear; it may, in fact, yield wonderful surprises. As we will see, amid all the technicalities of the ordinances in Leviticus, there are manifestations of grace that may be surprising to those who rarely tread this ground. For example, in the seemingly ordinary instructions of Leviticus 6:5 pertaining to illegitimately acquired property, we find such a manifestation of grace hidden behind apparently inconsequential details.

The broader context of our verse describes a variety of behaviors Israelites might engage in that require a guilt offering. These guilt-inducing behaviors include obtaining the property of someone else by illicit means such as denying that someone left something in your care, lying about receiving stolen goods, cheating someone out of their property, lying about finding lost property, or swearing falsely about these or similar activities. The legal penalty for any of these violations includes, in addition to a guilt offering, returning the wrongfully obtained property to its rightful owner along with an additional fifth of its value.

The provision seems reasonable and unremarkable, and we might read right over it without a second thought. But there is a hidden depth of meaning in this biblical law that we register only when we consider one of the details more closely. Let's look specifically at the curious detail requiring the offender to add a fifth of the value to the illegally obtained item before returning it. Why not ramp up this amount to a more generous 25 percent? Or why not make bookkeeping easier and reduce it to an even 10 percent? Why is any additional amount required at all? We can gain some help in answering these questions by examining the practices of Israel's ancient Near Eastern neighbors in this regard.

There are several ancient Near Eastern law collections that have survived to the present day, and like the biblical law collection in which our verse is found, they too contain provisions that deal with the issue of illegally obtained property. The penalties they prescribe for these kinds of infractions vary to a great degree. Some require the payment of a simple monetary fine (e.g., ten shekels for stealing a boat[1] or five shekels for stealing a plow[2]). Some of these law collections mandate physical punishment in addition to the payment of a fine (e.g., being flogged with staves[3] or the loss of a hand[4]). Some of these legal provisions even stipulate that the perpetrator must be put to death.[5] There are many factors that contribute to the variety of penalties, including the value of what was stolen, the status of the perpetrator (e.g., whether a slave or free person), the status of the real or perceived victim (e.g., whether a commoner, royal figure, one of the temple personnel, or a deity), and whether the stolen item had both value in itself and value based on what it could generate in the future, such as a bull, stallion, or seed. Clearly, the biblical legal materials contain nothing approaching this level of complexity. Any parallel our biblical verse may have to the ancient Near Eastern texts is not, therefore, to be found in the area of legal prescriptions regarding theft but in a different economic area altogether.

The legal pronouncements in ancient Near Eastern texts that *do* have closer correspondence to those in the biblical text belong surprisingly to the area of finance—in particular, the area of loans. In Babylonia, for example, the prescribed interest rate for loans of silver was 20 percent. This differs from the customary interest charged for loans of grain, which was 33 1/3 percent.[6] The 20 percent figure for loans of silver is intriguing because, as you may have noticed, it corresponds precisely to the figure of "a fifth of its value" found in our passage. This neat correspondence seems to be blurred, however, by the figure of 33 1/3 percent for grain loans. But the problem introduced by the difference between these two interest rates is more illusory than real. As W. F. Leemans, an expert in Babylonian legal and economic texts, has noted, "In the time of the dynasty of Hammurabi, just as during the earlier dynasty of Ur, the customary interest on grain *in private business* amounted to 33 1/3 percent and that on silver to 20 percent. The customary interest on barley-loans supplied *by temples* was probably 20 percent."[7] Moreover, "the different rates of interest for silver and grain may be more apparent than actual" due to the fact that "the interest rate for grain, which would seasonally depreciate, would be higher than the rate for silver, which did not depreciate, in order for the same profit to be realized by the creditor."[8] When these factors are taken into account, we can confidently conclude that the prevailing ancient Near Eastern interest rate was 20 percent.

This bit of financial detail from Israel's neighbors that may have initially seemed insignificant to us turns out to be the key to unlocking the hidden depths of meaning in our biblical verse. Contrary to the stipulations found in other ancient Near Eastern law collections, the Bible does not mandate that the discovered thief pay an exorbitant fine, be flogged with staves, have his hand cut off, or even be executed. Instead, the Bible offers grace in place of these harsh penalties. The biblical law expressed in Leviticus 6:5 essentially mandates that the victim graciously regard the temporary misappropriation of his goods *as a loan* (which accrues a 20 percent interest) rather than *as a theft*. In this way reconciliation with the aggrieved party can be achieved, just as the presentation of a guilt offering achieves reconciliation with God.

In connection with this gracious provision, we must also address the fact that Israelites were expressly forbidden to charge their fellow citizens interest on loans (Exod 22:25; Lev 25:35–37; Deut 23:20–21). So how can the law of Leviticus 6:5 (if it is mandating the payment of an amount equal to the prevailing interest rate) be reconciled with the prohibition against charging interest on loans? The answer to this question is that the victim has not actually made a loan. What *has* taken place instead is a theft that is being graciously treated as a loan. The victim is not charging any interest. Rather, Israel's divinely delivered legal prescriptions have graciously included a provision for creating the legal fiction of a loan so that the victim of the theft can be duly compensated for the temporary loss of his property, while the thief is allowed to repay an additional "fifth of its value" in lieu of the harsher penalties meted out by other ancient Near Eastern cultures. In this way the law is gracious to both parties. The victim receives compensation (similar to what would be received in a loan agreement in the surrounding cultures), and the thief's punishment is not as harsh (as it otherwise would be in the surrounding cultures). The provision of Leviticus 6:5 is in keeping with the Bible's prioritization of people over property and grace over gain. It enables relationships to be restored and shalom to be reestablished within the covenant community. Even in something as seemingly pedestrian as a legal response to theft, the depth of God's grace once again surfaces.

At the beginning of this chapter, we saw that understanding the laws that Jesus fulfills helps us to become more like him. In Leviticus 6:5, God provides a gracious alternative to judgment. The ultimate expression of such divine provision is the gracious alternative to judgment God provides for wrongdoers in Jesus Christ. Through faith, instead of the death our sins deserve, we are graciously granted "eternal life in Christ Jesus our Lord" (Rom 6:23). We become more like Jesus when we respond to offenses against us with the same grace we ourselves have received from God. As the apostle Paul put it in his letter to the church at Ephesus, "Follow God's example, therefore, as dearly loved children and walk in the way of love, just as Christ loved us" (Eph 5:1–2).

THINGS TO CONSIDER

1. God has reconciled believers to himself in Christ, "not counting people's sin against them" (2 Cor 5:19). Consider how God's gracious provision for the thief in Leviticus

6:1–5 reflects his gracious provision of Jesus Christ. Do you think the thief deserved the grace extended to him? Do you think we deserve the grace extended to us in Christ?

2. In the Lord's Prayer, we pray that God would "forgive us our debts, as we also have forgiven our debtors" (Matt 6:12). In what ways could your treatment of others reflect the forgiveness you have received from God? What wrongs do you have the hardest time forgiving?

3. The biblical provision for the treatment of a thief was strikingly different from the treatment a thief could expect in the surrounding cultures. Does your treatment of other believers, even those who have wronged you (by stealing from you or otherwise mistreating you), differ from the way unbelievers treat one another? How does this behavior advance or hinder the gospel message?

8

—o—

Enduring Witnesses

This day I call the heavens and the earth as
witnesses against you that I have set before
you life and death, blessings and curses.
—Deuteronomy 30:19

A quick search through the trial records in the law libraries of Harvard, Princeton, and Yale reveals the absence of heaven and earth on the witness lists for any court proceedings. And yet near the end of the book of Deuteronomy, in 30:19, we encounter exactly that. God, through his servant Moses, has been laying out the specifics of his legal, covenant relationship with his people. Why heaven and earth would be subpoenaed at this point is a mystery. And how they could ever function as witnesses is equally mystifying. We might suspect, therefore, that something more is going on here than we're aware of. In other words, this seems like one of those verses that has a deeper meaning worth exploring!

To begin uncovering the surprising significance of this verse, we must first go back about thirty-five hundred years to the period of the Hittite Empire, which reached the height of its power from the fifteenth to the twelfth centuries BC[1]— during the time when the Israelites were entering the promised land and establishing their dominance there. While the Hittites, who inhabited an area north of Israel that includes modern-day Turkey, are worthy of study in their own right, what is most relevant for our purposes is the form of the treaties this powerful nation (suzerain) made with subordinate (vassal) states. The benefits the suzerain nation would provide for its vassal states and the vassals' responsibilities to their suzerain overlord were spelled out in the treaties they both agreed to. These so-called suzerain-vassal treaties had a fixed form that includes the following parts:

1. **A historical prologue**—a history of the past relationship between the powerful king and those who were entering into a more formal relationship with him.

   This feature served to provide the basis or foundation of the relationship going forward. If the king had been gracious in the past, there was every reason to expect he would continue to be so in the future.

2. **Stipulations**—the heart of the treaty, outlining the kind of behavior the powerful king required and what could be expected of him in return.

   Gracious behavior on the part of the king deserved to be reciprocated by that of his subjects. Their responsibility was to live in a way that would advance their relationship with the king and reject anything that would threaten it.

3. **Blessings**—a description of the benefits that would accrue to those who followed the stipulations of the treaty.

   Within their relationship with the king, his subjects could expect his care, protection, and provision.

4. **Curses**—a description of the negative consequences that could be expected for failure to follow the stipulations of the treaty.

   Rejecting the relationship with the one who provides care, protection, and provision would necessarily result in isolation, vulnerability, and want.

5. **Witnesses**—third parties present at the initiation of the treaty between the powerful king and those entering into the formal relationship with him.

   Witnesses were listed so that they could be summoned in the future should there be a need to corroborate the mutually agreed upon terms of the relationship, as well as the violation or fulfillment of those terms.

Many biblical scholars recognize these elements as forming the outline to the book of Deuteronomy, which details the covenant relationship God makes with his people.[2] The Israelites who received this revelation, therefore, would have understood Deuteronomy as an example of a suzerain-vassal treaty, with God as the suzerain and his people as the vassal state.

Thus, the first part of the treaty form, the historical prologue, is recognized in Deuteronomy 1:6–4:43. In this section, Moses reminds the Israelites of everything God has done for them in the past—things that prove his love for them, give them confidence in his continued care for them in the future, and motivate their loving response to him.

The stipulations, the second part of the treaty form, are recognized as comprising the bulk of Deuteronomy, extending from 4:44 to 26:19.[3] In this section, Moses encourages God's people to live in a way that fulfills God's expectations and intentions for them. In other words, Moses encourages them to live in a way that nurtures their relationship with God and leads them to a fuller experience of the life he desires for them.

The blessings, the third part of the treaty form, are found in 28:1–14, where Moses spells out for the Israelites "all these blessings" that they would experience if they "fully obey the LORD . . . and carefully follow all his commands" (28:1–2).

The curses, the fourth part of the treaty form, are presented in 28:15–58. In these verses, Moses makes it clear that if the Israelites reject God's path of life prescribed by the stipulations, "all these curses will come on [them] and overtake [them]" (28:15).

Finally, we come to a consideration of the last part of the suzerain-vassal treaty: the witnesses. Perhaps surprisingly, we also encounter witnesses in Deuteronomy. In the non-Israelite ancient Near Eastern cultures, various gods were often called as witnesses. After all, the witnesses would have to be as enduring as the treaty relationship was expected to be. The witnesses had to be perpetually on hand to verify the existence of and adherence to the treaty. Of course, these false gods of other ancient Near Eastern cultures would not do as witnesses for any relationship the true God had established. Instead of these fictions, God calls the most enduring features of creation to serve as witnesses. He says, "This day I call the heavens and the earth as witnesses against you that I have set before you life and death" (30:19). As long as the heavens and the earth endure, therefore, there will be witnesses to the fact and terms of this divine-human relationship.

Before we consider the profound implications associated with these unusual witnesses, we must take a moment to acknowledge the sad history of human failure in this (or any) divine-human relationship. Simply put, human beings cannot remain faithful to God (i.e., fulfill the terms of our relationship with him). Perhaps the clearest expression of this depressing truth is provided by the apostle Paul, who hammers away at the topic of human faithlessness like a relentless prosecuting attorney presenting his closing argument to the jury:

> There is no one righteous, not even one;
>> there is no one who understands;
>> there is no one who seeks God.
> All have turned away,
>> they have together become worthless;
> there is no one who does good,
>> not even one. (Rom 3:10–12)

Paul makes it abundantly clear that there is no hope for any of us to fulfill the relational obligations of the covenant relationship God has set forth in the book of Deuteronomy. This fact should drive all of us to the edge of despair because, as Moses has stated, true life can be found only within that relationship (Deut 30:19–20). And brokenness, pain, suffering, and death await everyone who is not in such a relationship with God. Human beings, on their own, are at an impossible impasse. But with incomprehensible grace, God has chosen to do something about this. And, indeed, that is our only hope.

In an incredible act of mercy and love, God himself became a human being to do what none of us could. Jesus came to fulfill on our behalf the relational obligations that God set forth through Moses. Those who claim Jesus as their representative have his perfect life credited to them so that they may now enjoy the relational blessings that have been promised for such a life! But what about the relational curses for previous failures on our part? These are not simply ignored or dismissed. These crimes must be paid for. And Jesus did this too. On the cross, Jesus experienced God's judgment on every human offense against God—even though Jesus himself had merited none of it. So everyone who claims Jesus as their representative has him now representing them in both obedience and judgment. His obedience counts for them, and his experience of God's judgment counts for them. This isn't just good news; it's wonderful news! But how can we be sure it's true?

Who could we turn to for reliable testimony that all the formal relationship obligations with God have truly been fulfilled? Who else but the enduring witnesses—heaven and earth? These parties to the relationship were present when the terms of the relationship were finally and perfectly fulfilled, even though the other momentous events of that day may have obscured their testimony.

The book of Matthew tells us that at Jesus's crucifixion, first the heavens gave their testimony by becoming dark: "From noon until three in the afternoon darkness came over all the land" (Matt 27:45). Then the earth gave its testimony as well: "The earth shook, the rocks split and the tombs broke open" (27:51–52). The heavens and the earth, these ancient, enduring witnesses to the divine-human relationship, testified that its terms had been perfectly fulfilled by the only human being who could do so—God himself in human flesh. Those who by faith claim Jesus as their representative can be just as confident in the security of their relationship with God as they can be in the faithfulness of Jesus. The profound importance of these witnesses to the relationship between God and his people finally comes to light and adds clarity and confidence to our understanding of the greatest event in human history.

THINGS TO CONSIDER

1. Jesus has perfectly carried out all the requirements (i.e., the stipulations) of the covenant. So do the laws of Deuteronomy have any significance for believers today? What were those laws intended to achieve? How does that relate to what Christ offers believers? Do any relational obligations remain for believers to fulfill? What happens if believers don't fulfill them?

2. The historical prologue always preceded the stipulations in the ancient suzerain-vassal treaties. How does God's history with you motivate your faithfulness to him? Is God ever unfaithful? How do you explain Jesus's crying out "My God, my God, why have you forsaken me?" (Matt 27:46).

3. The heavens and the earth testified that Jesus's life and death satisfied all the terms of God's covenant relationship with human beings. Does their testimony strengthen your faith? Can you explain why?

9

—∘—

BE CAREFUL WHAT
YOU ASK FOR

*"You will realize what an evil thing
you did in the eyes of the LORD
when you asked for a king."*
—1 SAMUEL 12:17

U nlike today, when names are often chosen primarily for
the way they sound, their conformity to what names are
culturally trending, or to preserve a name in family tradition, in
the Old Testament, names meant something. As biblical scholar
Raymond Abba put it, "In biblical thought a name is not a mere
label of identification; it is an expression of the essential nature of
its bearer. A [person's] name reveals [their] character."[1] At times
in the Bible, this connection between a person's name and their
character is made explicit. For example, when Jacob tricks his

brother Esau out of getting the blessing of the firstborn son, Esau cries out, "Isn't he rightly named Jacob? This is the second time he has taken advantage of me: He took my birthright, and now he's taken my blessing!" (Gen 27:36). To catch the connection Esau is making here, we need to realize that he's associating the name "Jacob" in Hebrew (יַעֲקֹב *ya'ăqōb*) with the verb translated "has taken advantage of me" (יַעֲקֹב *ya'ăqōb*) to make the point that Jacob is acting according to the meaning of his name. Later, Abigail, in reference to her husband, makes a similar connection between the meaning of a name and the character of the person who bears it. She says to David, "Please pay no attention, my lord, to that wicked man Nabal. He is just like his name—his name means Fool, and folly goes with him" (1 Sam 25:25).

Considering biblical characters in this light is fascinating, but what relevance does it have, you might be thinking, to 1 Samuel 12:17, the verse we are considering in this chapter? After all, it contains no names. True enough, but it does play on the meaning of the name of the person it alludes to. Because the person the Israelites got when they asked for a king was Saul. And it is the significance of his name that gives deeper meaning to this verse.

But before we explore this hidden meaning a bit further, we should make sure we understand the context of 1 Samuel 12:17. In the chapters just preceding this verse, the Israelites have made a momentous decision. After decades of being ruled sporadically by judges, who were raised up by God to meet specific challenges his people faced, the Israelites decided the time had come for them to have a more long-term ruler over all the tribes. More specifically, they asked Samuel for "a king to lead us, such as all the other nations have" (8:5).

This might not seem so alarming. After all, hundreds of

years earlier Moses had already anticipated Israel's desire for a king. Before they had even entered the promised land, he told them, "When you enter the land the LORD your God is giving you and have taken possession of it and settled in it, and you say, 'Let us set a king over us like all the nations around us,' be sure to appoint over you a king the LORD your God chooses" (Deut 17:14–15). And we might consider the establishment of a monarchy to be the next logical step in Israel's evolution as a nation. But there is more going on here than a simple request for a king. We need to look again carefully at 1 Samuel 8:5. In that verse, the final clause changes the complexion of the entire event. The Israelites did not simply ask for a king; they asked for a king "such as all the other nations have."

This was not the way it was supposed to be! Israel had been called by God to be unique among the nations. They had been chosen from all the people on earth to demonstrate to the rest of the world a new kind of humanity that found its security and significance, its meaning and purpose in its relationship with God. They were supposed to be a beacon of light to the Gentiles (Isa 42:6; 49:6). In other words, they were supposed to show all the other nations the way to a richer, fuller life in relationship with God. But at this point the exact opposite seems to have taken place. The Israelites asked to become like the other nations instead of living in a way that would cause the nations to want to become like them. How discouraging this must have been to God! His specially chosen, guided, delivered, and blessed people had renounced their very purpose as God's people. As God himself says, they had rejected him as their king in favor of a human king (1 Sam 8:7).

God yielded to their request and granted them a king. But

things didn't go so well for this first king. Saul seemed to start out on the right foot, expressing an appropriate humility when Samuel told him he would be king (9:21). But after he had been anointed as king to the cheers of "Long live the king!" (10:24), it didn't take long for the power of the kingship to go to his head and lead him to overstep his bounds. About two years later, in a battle with the Philistines that was not going his way, Saul made a grave error in judgment. Hard-pressed, afraid, seeing his troops scatter, and weary of waiting for Samuel's arrival, Saul felt compelled to, and decided he had the right to, present offerings to the Lord (13:8–9)—a function reserved for priests alone, which of course Saul was not. When Samuel arrived, just as Saul was tidying up after the burnt offering, Samuel pronounced Saul's judgment. As a consequence of Saul's wrongful act, God would take the kingship away from him. Samuel went on to say that in Saul's place, "the Lord has sought out a man after his own heart and appointed him ruler of his people" (13:14). What an ignominious end to Israel's first efforts at a monarchy!

So where did the Israelites go wrong? And what deeper meaning lies hidden in the seemingly ordinary words of 12:17? Even though there doesn't seem to be anything intrinsically wrong with the establishment of a monarchy, this episode involving Saul presents us with a remarkable contrast between two approaches in accomplishing it. The Israelites decided to take the first steps toward a monarchy on their own, without seeking any guidance from God, and instead used the model of the nations around them as their guide. But their idea of a king was strikingly different from the Lord's idea. We are told that the Lord wanted someone after his own heart; the Israelites asked for someone "such as all the other nations have" (8:5).

But wait, there's more! The author ingeniously used the names of Israel's first two kings to indicate the fundamental difference between these two approaches to establishing the monarchy. This is the greater depth of meaning that 12:17 is communicating. Saul, the kind of king the Israelites asked for, represents the first, unsuccessful approach to kingship. In Hebrew, Saul's name (Hebrew: *šā'ûl*) is spelled using the Hebrew consonants for *š*, ', and *l*. The Hebrew word for "ask" (*šā'al*) is spelled with exactly the same three consonants! Notice how the bolded consonants in the following table are the same for these two words.

Saul	*šā'ûl*
ask	*šā'al*

In Hebrew, the pattern of the vowels and consonants in Saul's name communicates a passive nuance to this verb. So Saul's name means "the asked-for one." Now we can see the hidden significance and appropriateness of Saul's name. He is the one the Israelites "asked for." In addition to our verse, this play on the meaning of Saul's name and the verb "ask" is made a few other times in this part of the book of 1 Samuel:

1. "Samuel told all the words of the LORD to the people who were asking [*š-'-l*] him for a king" (8:10).
2. "Now here is the king you have chosen, the one you asked [*š-'-l*] for" (12:13).
3. "We have added to all our other sins the evil of asking [*š-'-l*] for a king" (12:19).

By repeatedly making the connection between the verb "ask" and Saul's name, the author is reminding the Israelites that King Saul is just the kind of king they asked for. He is the king "such as all the other nations have" (8:5), one who rules by his own judgment instead of under the direction of God. Their predicament reminds us of the proverb "Be careful what you ask for; you just might get it." The Israelites certainly got the kind of king they asked for, and he turned out to be a disaster for them.

In contrast to the kind of king the people asked for (Saul, "the asked-for one"), the Lord chose "a man after his own heart" (13:14). The Lord's choice was David, whose name means "beloved." And David, the one loved by God, would turn out to be a much better king than Saul, the one asked for by the Israelites. If only the Israelites had sought God's choice from the beginning, they could have avoided the problems Saul brought to the nation. But it always seems easier to do what is right in our own eyes first. And God appears willing to allow us to experience the negative consequences of doing that so we'll be much more ready and willing to follow his lead afterward.

As in Israel's misguided request for a king, all of us forget, at times, that God's ways are better than our ways (Isa 55:8–9). He knows far more than we ever could, and he has communicated to us the best way a human being can live. But we so often ignore his divine wisdom and prefer instead to be guided by our limited human perspective. This is the essence of sin, which encourages us to place more importance on our own desires and understanding than on God's. The Israelites had asked for a king that conformed to their own understanding of what a good king should be instead of a king after God's own heart—that is, one who conformed to God's understanding of what a good king should be. And we similarly often choose what we want over what God prefers. In the prophet Isaiah's words,

> We all, like sheep, have gone astray,
>> each of us has turned to our own way;
> and the LORD has laid on him
>> the iniquity of us all. (Isa 53:6)

With us, as with the Israelites, turning to our own way has resulted in broken lives, broken relationships, and separation from God. But the ultimate Davidic king, the one after God's own heart, the beloved Son with whom God is well pleased (Matt 3:17), has paid the price for all these bad choices in our lives. He invites us to enjoy life under the pleasant rule of a gracious king instead of the tyrants we choose for ourselves.

THINGS TO CONSIDER

1. If you were an Israelite during the time of Samuel (without knowing the end of this biblical story), which person would you want to be king over your nation: Saul, "as handsome a young man as could be found anywhere in Israel, and . . . a head taller than anyone else" (1 Sam 9:2), or David, a shepherd and the youngest son of Jesse (16:11)? Which do you value more in others, external characteristics or internal ones?

2. What are some negative consequences of making decisions that rely entirely on your own understanding, without

seeking God's guidance in prayer or his Word? Do you really believe God knows the best way for you to live? If so, how does your belief that God's wisdom is greater than yours show up in practical ways in your life?

3. What does it mean to live under the rule of King Jesus? How would you describe this kind of life to a new believer? Does it mean we never get to choose what we want to do anymore? Or conversely, can we choose to do whatever we want and still call Jesus our king? Does our faith require obedience to anyone or anything? Or would that requirement confuse law with grace?

10

—o—

AROUND THE
GLASSY SEA

*He made the Sea of cast metal, circular
in shape, measuring ten cubits from rim
to rim and five cubits high. It took a line
of thirty cubits to measure around it.*
—1 KINGS 7:23

The book of 1 Kings is certainly a region of the Bible that most Christians seldom explore. One doesn't hear too many devotions, sermons, or reflections on its contents, much less any kind of discussion regarding the specifics of the objects associated with the temple. In 1 Kings 7:23, for example, we are introduced to an object called "the Sea." If there is any deeper meaning associated with this clunky metal fixture, it is well and truly hidden! What possible surprising significance, we might understandably ask, could there be to the description of this piece of temple furniture that has lain unattended among the many other long-neglected furnishings in the dusty attic of 1 Kings? It may surprise you to learn that there is, in fact, immense significance. There is indeed much to see about the Sea! But that hidden depth of meaning can be uncovered only after we investigate a little deeper into a particular area of Israel's ancient Near Eastern context. Before we go poking around in the neighbors' backyards to see what information we can glean there, let's first remind ourselves of what the Sea was.

The Sea was essentially a massive basin. It was made of cast bronze about fifteen feet in diameter and held about twelve thousand gallons of water. It was located near the entrance of the temple and had the practical purpose of providing the water necessary for the many priestly washings associated with the temple rituals (cf. 2 Chr 4:6). But its name and location reveal a deeper significance that is not immediately obvious to most contemporary Bible readers. Why was this large basin called "the Sea"? And why did it have to be put in a specific place in the temple court? To begin to grasp the deeper significance of these details, we now need to consider how the sea was regarded in other ancient Near Eastern cultures.

Understandably, ancient cultures feared the sea. A host of unseen dangers lurked in its inky depths, and its waves could turn from mild to menacing in a matter of minutes. Anyone who has spent any time on the open sea during storms knows the incredible and terrifying power these meteorological nightmares can unleash. I've been in a submarine in the North Atlantic during one of these storms. We were a hundred and fifty feet below the surface of the sea and were *still* taking twenty-degree rolls.

The size and power that the waves on the surface must have had in order for their effects to extend so far down into the depths was unimaginable. And these devastating storms can reach inland for hundreds of miles. The magnitude of their potential destructive force is staggering to contemplate and horrifying to experience. Hurricane winds can reach speeds of up to two hundred miles per hour and release the energy of an atomic bomb every two seconds![1] The biblical accounts of storms at sea that Jonah (Jonah 1:4–15) and the apostle Paul (Acts 27:13–44) experienced only underscore the threat that people along the coast felt from that quarter.

Psalm 107 describes the terrifying experience of those who "went out on the sea [םָי yām] in ships" and found themselves in the midst of one of these storms:

> They saw the works of the LORD,
> > his wonderful deeds in the deep.
> For he spoke and stirred up a tempest
> > that lifted high the waves.
> They mounted up to the heavens and went down
> > to the depths;
> > in their peril their courage melted away.
> They reeled and staggered like drunkards;
> > they were at their wits' end.
> Then they cried out to the LORD in their trouble,
> > and he brought them out of their distress.
> > (Ps 107:24–28)

Contrary to the biblical conviction that the Lord is in complete control of the sea that he himself has created (Ps 95:5), "Near

Eastern mythologies describe the sea as a force of chaos that only the most powerful deity could constrain."[2] In fact, in the Canaanite culture of Ugarit (a city-state situated along the coast of the Mediterranean just north of Israel), the sea garnered such fear and respect that it was elevated to the status of a deity (named Yam, as in Ps 107, the common Semitic word for "sea"). And because the appeasement of the god of the unruly waters of the sea was regarded as vitally important for the maintenance of the maritime commerce in the seaport of Ugarit, Yam had a cult there and received regular offerings.[3]

Though the biblical authors never suggest that Israel elevated the sea to the status of a deity, they nevertheless regarded it as an unpredictable and deadly chaotic power that perpetually threatened to unravel the fabric of the created order, resulting in the loss of life, safety, and property. This cultural association of the sea with destructive chaos persisted down through the ages and is also present in the New Testament and the symbology it contains. "In fact, the evil world powers and the antichrist of the last days which oppose God and his people are symbolized as beasts arising from the sea (Dan 7:3; Rev 13:1)."[4]

It is against this background understanding of the perceived nature of the sea that we can begin to understand the larger significance of the Sea among the temple furnishings. The inclusion of this article of furniture in the temple complex, situated as it was before the earthly throne of the God of Israel, tacitly communicated to Israel the fact that the sea was under God's control, not the other way around. No matter how terrifying was the power that the sea could unleash against human beings, the power of God is far greater. What better way to picture that reality than to have the Sea present not in its chaotic fury but in the quiet stillness appropriate in the presence of its almighty divine master and maker? The Sea no longer threatens life but rather holds water for the ritual washings of the priests who make sacrifices to the Lord of life.

This imagery of God subduing the sea, and the chaos associated with it, reappears throughout the Bible. Already in the account of creation in the book of Genesis, we find a dark, "formless and empty," watery world in which chaos reigns (Gen 1:2). By the exercise of God's creative power, that chaos is systematically addressed as the world is progressively changed into an orderly place that is "very good" (1:31). This orderliness remains until sin appears and reintroduces a measure of the primeval chaos—although by God's grace not to the fullest extent possible. And the day when God will finally and entirely eliminate the damage and disorder of sin is pictured in terms of the sea as well. In the apostle John's vision of that time, he sees God bringing about the culmination of his redemptive program while before him is "a sea of glass, clear as crystal" (Rev 4:6; 15:2). At that time, the sea no longer dares to rise up in the presence of God but is subdued so completely that not a single ripple disturbs its placid surface. It is as still as glass. It has been changed from a churning maelstrom of destructive power to a quieted and submissive servant. But God's subjugation of the sea goes even further! At the consummation of God's redemption, there will be "a new heaven and a new earth," where there is "no longer any sea" at all (21:1). In other words, there will be "no more death or mourning or crying or pain" (21:4) caused by sin and represented by the chaotic sea. Instead, there will be abundant life and healing and joy represented by its opposite: "the spring of the water of life" (21:6). Even before that glorious day, when God's people must "walk through the darkest valley," he leads them "beside quiet waters" (Ps 23:2, 4) as they do so.

The Sea, with its thousands of gallons of quiet water, sitting before the presence of God in his temple, provided a clear object lesson for all who saw it: No matter what chaotic situation they may face, the one true God is mightier and is still in control. As the old hymn puts it, "Though the wrong seems oft so strong, God is the ruler yet."[5] Who knew that there was such treasure to be found behind this bulky and often ignored piece of temple furniture?

THINGS TO CONSIDER

1. The Israelites could hardly imagine any earthly force more powerful than the Mediterranean Sea to their west. And yet the glassy stillness of the Sea among the temple furnishings signifies that even this powerful force is impotent in the presence of an omnipotent God. What is the most fearsome force in your life? Do you believe God is more powerful?

2. The Israelites had the object lesson of the huge basin called the Sea to remind them of God's power and authority over a world that often seemed out of control. What object lesson do you have today to remind you that God still reigns in the midst of apparent chaos? Does the image of the cross accomplish this for you?

3. The waters of chaos and death are ultimately replaced by living water that comes from Jesus (John 4:10) and those

who believe in him (7:38). In light of what you've learned about the symbolism of the Sea, what does God's living water mean for you in practical terms? Has it calmed any storms in your life?

11

—o—

THE LAST STRAW

"My father made your yoke heavy;
I will make it even heavier."
—1 KINGS 12:14

We have all heard people in difficult situations only dig their hole deeper by continuing to talk. This is what we find in the verse we'll be exploring in this chapter. The words of King Rehoboam recorded in 1 Kings 12:14 are not something anyone would want to hear from their new monarch. This unwelcome, heartless, and ultimately politically suicidal statement was uttered by Rehoboam mere days after he had been installed as king following the death of his father, King Solomon. On their surface, his words are already digging a deep hole for him. They effectively and unmistakably communicate the harsh attitude of this new king toward his Israelite subjects. Sadly, there is a further depth of cruelty that Rehoboam is digging with his words and actions that an awareness of a common practice of Israel's ancient Near Eastern neighbors will reveal. But before considering that broader context, let's review the more immediate context of Israel's historical situation.

Israel was a relatively young monarchy. At this point in their history, we may have expected to read about a continuation of the upward trajectory of the progress they had enjoyed for the last eighty years under the reigns of David and Solomon. But everything would change with this official proclamation of King Rehoboam. That's not to say, however, that things were entirely rosy for the Israelites before this time, even during the illustrious reign of King Solomon. This reality is already indicated by what is said in the first half of our verse: "My father [i.e., Solomon] made your yoke heavy."

The Israelite populace had indeed been subjected to a variety of burdensome governmental regulations during Solomon's kingship. He had divided the kingdom into twelve administrative regions that were overseen by district governors. These official functionaries were required to supply provisions for the king and his household on a twelve-month rotation (4:7). And these provisions were not insignificant. During their month of responsibility each year, each administrative region had to supply 900 cors (about 165 tons) of the finest flour, 1,800 cors (about 330 tons) of meal, 300 head of stall-fed cattle, 3,000 sheep and goats, as well as deer, gazelles, roebucks, choice fowl, and barley and straw for the horses (4:22–23). It is not hard to imagine the growing resentment against the royal house that was fueled by such a huge burden placed on the citizenry. But even with the forbearing compliance of its people in this regard, the demands of the bloated monarchic bureaucracy were still not satisfied.

King Solomon not only required the people to provide his administration with a significant amount of their possessions, he also required them to provide him with themselves! The Bible records that for his extensive building projects, Solomon "conscripted laborers from all Israel" (5:13). The word translated here as "laborers" (מַס *mas*) refers more specifically to *forced* labor, "approaching the conditions of slavery."[1] The labor was unpaid and lasted as long as the state decided it would. And King Solomon decided that his citizens would be subjected to that unpaid, forced labor for one month out of every three (5:14), although it is not clear whether this was a standard duration or applied specifically to the temple building project involving thirty thousand men (5:13). Whatever the duration, that such a governmental imposition was exceedingly onerous to the Israelites is indicated by the fact that they later stoned to death Adoniram, the man Solomon had placed in charge of their forced labor (5:14; 2 Chr 10:18).[2]

It is no wonder, then, that the people would request from their new king, Rehoboam, that he lessen their heavy burden. A citizenry that was already straining under the load of governmental taxes, regulations, and compulsory service could only be pushed so far. Notice that King Rehoboam did not deny that the basis of his people's appeal was true. He admitted that his father had indeed made their yoke heavy. But instead of securing the immediate goodwill of his people by responding favorably to their request and reducing their burden, he rashly decided that he was going to make it even heavier. We can already understand how such a statement by King Rehoboam would push the people's frustration past the breaking point. It was the last straw. But an awareness of a custom regularly observed by Israel's ancient

Near Eastern neighbors helps us to more fully appreciate the depth of their crushed expectations.

There is documentary evidence from cultures surrounding Israel that it was common practice for a king, especially at the beginning of his reign, to initiate reforms intended to bring about some measure of socioeconomic relief to his people. For the Babylonians, this was known as a *mîšarum*, a term having the general meaning of "justice" but also referring to a formal royal proclamation intended to effect justice in society and "remedy certain economic malfunctions."[3] Biblical and ancient Near East scholar J. J. Finkelstein explains its purpose: "A *mîšarum*-act is mainly characterized by measures designed to remit . . . certain types of obligations and indebtedness. . . . The remissive acts, enacted first at the beginning of a reign and possibly afterwards as well if the situation warranted, were acknowledged as among the important accomplishments of a king. . . ."[4]

History has preserved for us an example of such a *mîšarum*. It was promulgated by Ammiṣaduqa, the tenth ruler of the Hammurabi Dynasty in Babylon (1646–1626 BC),[5] and its provisions include the forgiveness of debts, restrictions on creditors, and freedom for certain kinds of slaves. In the edict itself, the king describes himself as "Ammiṣaduqa the king, [the god] Enlil having magnified his noble lordship, like [the god] Shamash he rose forth in steadfastness over his country, and instituted justice for the whole of his people."[6]

A similar concern for socioeconomic justice is evident among the Hittites in the Edict of Tudḫaliya IV (1265–1240 BC).[7] Regarding the rationale for this royal decree, Raymond Westbrook and Roger D. Woodard, specialists in ancient Near Eastern and biblical law, note, "The ostensible motivation was religious: by reestablishing equity and ending abuses the ruler pleases the god of justice and thereby secures the legitimacy of his reign. It is clear, therefore, why a ruler would begin his reign with such a decree."[8]

Both the Babylonian and Hittite kings began their reigns, therefore, with declarations of much-anticipated and appreciated relief from economic oppression. Moreover, these declarations were also intended to please their gods, especially those gods associated with justice. In his first opportunity to promulgate similar reforms for his people, Rehoboam did not consult the God of justice, who had delivered the entire nation from the injustice of slavery in Egypt. Instead, he followed the advice of "the young men who had grown up with him" (1 Kgs 12:8, 10). In doing so, he displayed a contempt for his people that was even beneath that of his ancient Near Eastern neighbors, who did not know the Lord.

As the king of God's people, Rehoboam was responsible to set an example for his people (and the surrounding nations) in manifesting the attributes of the God they served—such attributes as compassion, care, and justice. However, Rehoboam not only demonstrated a shocking lack of these attributes, but his obstinate mercilessness also presented to his people a picture of God that was exactly the opposite of what would be expected of a merciful and gracious Lord. The deeper significance of this verse is that Rehoboam's callous response to his beleaguered people not only violated his official responsibilities but also went against the widespread practice of newly inaugurated kings in the ancient Near East, whose first acts (and subsequent continuing responsibilities) were expected to (and did) include the ameliorating actions such as those the Israelites were requesting from their new king.

So it is no surprise that Rehoboam's coldhearted obstinacy was the last straw that led to the permanent division of the kingdom. With rare exceptions, the following kings did not do much better with their royal responsibilities. The history of Israel from this point forward is discouraging. It would take almost another millennium for a Davidic king to arise who would finally give God's people the answer they sought from Rehoboam. Jesus said to them, "Come to me, all you who are weary and burdened, and I will give you rest. Take my yoke upon you and learn from me, for I am gentle and humble in heart, and you will find rest for your souls. For my yoke is easy and my burden is light" (Matt 11:28–30).

THINGS TO CONSIDER

1. King Rehoboam allowed his inexperienced friends to persuade him to go against the advice of the experienced elders who had served his father. What might have motivated him to do this? Have you ever been similarly motivated to go along with your friends instead of following the advice of those who knew better?

2. Because of Rehoboam's rejection of their appeal, ten tribes rejected him as their king and chose Jeroboam as their king instead. However, Jeroboam led those tribes into idolatry and ultimate ruin. How should the church today respond to leaders who abuse their authority like Rehoboam? How can the church avoid the error of following contemporary Jeroboams?

3. Jesus said he "did not come to be served, but to serve, and to give his life as a ransom for many" (Matt 20:28). What does following the leadership model of Jesus (instead of that of Rehoboam) look like as you exercise leadership in your family, business, community, or church?

12

—o—

A BIRD IN A CAGE

*That night the angel of the LORD went out
and put to death a hundred and eighty-
five thousand in the Assyrian camp.*
—2 KINGS 19:35

To say the night described in 2 Kings 19:35 was not a good one for the Assyrians would be a severe understatement. The death toll is hard to fathom. It seems comparable to that produced by a nuclear bomb! And it is exactly the opposite of what everyone would have expected. No one could have imagined that Assyria would suffer such a loss, especially on this scale. But that this disastrous reversal of fortune indeed happened is corroborated by the Assyrians themselves. Before we look at this surprising extrabiblical support, however, we need to zoom out a little so that we can get some orientation to what is going on here.

The year was 701 BC. The leader of one of the mightiest

military forces the world had ever known was setting his sights on the Southern Kingdom of Judah. And humanly speaking, there was absolutely no reason to hope that the comparatively tiny nation of Judah could withstand the terrifying onslaught of the massive and well-equipped army of the Neo-Assyrian Empire. In fact, just a couple of decades earlier, in 722 BC, it had rolled over the Northern Kingdom of Israel with as little difficulty as an eighteen-wheeler barreling over a hapless squirrel that makes the fatal mistake of getting in its way. Now the Northern Kingdom of Israel was scattered to the winds, and the Assyrian war machine, under the capable leadership of King Sennacherib, was on the very doorstep of Judah! The consequences of an attack were terrifying to consider, not only because of the gross power mismatch but also because of how Assyria had regularly exercised that power. Nahum 3:1 describes Nineveh, the capital of Assyria, as "the city of blood, full of lies, full of plunder, never without victims!" In order to scare into submission any other kingdom who would dare to even entertain the notion of turning against them, the Assyrian army perpetrated the most horrendous atrocities imaginable against those who opposed them. These included skinning or dismembering live human beings and displaying the skins or heads of the victims on city walls, trees, or on stakes their friends were forced to parade throughout town.[1]

It is perfectly understandable, then, that King Ahaz of Judah, who had witnessed the crushing defeat of the kingdom of Israel just to his north at the hands of this seemingly invincible force, would seek to avoid a similar fate for his people by pledging his allegiance to the ruthless Assyrian king who led those forces. He was willing to do this even though it involved humiliating himself and his nation, as recounted in 2 Kings 16:7. Ahaz sent messengers to the Assyrian king, saying, "I am your servant and vassal." To further prove his submission, Ahaz "took the silver and gold found in the temple of the LORD and in the treasuries of the royal palace and sent it as a gift to the king of Assyria" (16:8).

And as if this shameful looting of the Lord's temple weren't enough, Ahaz did something even more unthinkable. After meeting with the king of Assyria personally, Ahaz replaced the bronze altar that stood before the Lord with a new altar of foreign design and then presented sacrilegious offerings on it. His further violations of the Lord's temple included disassembling its basins, replacing the bronze base of its large basin (called the Sea) with a stone one, taking away its Sabbath canopy, and removing its royal entryway. All these things Ahaz did "in deference to the king of Assyria" (16:17–18). It appeared to all the world as though both Judah and the God of Judah (who was apparently incapable or unwilling to do anything about it) were subject to the authority of the mighty Assyrian king.

Then Ahaz died and his son, Hezekiah, succeeded him as king of Judah. Unlike his father, Hezekiah was committed to the Lord. He would never dishonor God by pledging allegiance to a foreign king. So Hezekiah bravely "rebelled against the king of Assyria and did not serve him" (18:7). This was truly a case of David and Goliath on an international level! There was no way Assyria was going to let this insubordination go unaddressed.

So "in the fourteenth year of King Hezekiah's reign [701 BC], Sennacherib king of Assyria attacked all the fortified cities of Judah and captured them" (18:13). It looked like all was lost, and at this critical point of national peril, Hezekiah's faith wavered. He promised to pay Sennacherib whatever he wanted if only he would stop attacking Judah. In response, Sennacherib exacted from him thirty talents (about one ton) of gold and three hundred talents (about eleven tons) of silver (18:14–16). But as is always the case in making a deal with the devil, the devil cheats. He *is* the devil, after all. Sennacherib continued his attack despite Hezekiah's payment and turned the sights of his massive military machine toward Jerusalem itself, the capital city of Judah.

The odds against Hezekiah could not have been greater or the scales more imbalanced in Sennacherib's favor. Every one of Hezekiah's outlying, fortified cities had been overtaken. Jerusalem was the only fortified city that remained. There Hezekiah cowered and considered his next move. And thankfully his next move was the right one. He went into the temple of the Lord and laid his situation before God and also appealed to the prophet Isaiah (19:1–4; 2 Chr 32:20; Isa 37:1–4).

Then the difference between what is real and what is only apparent became clear. The haughty Assyrian king had defied the king of heaven and earth for long enough! God unleashed his agent of doom—the angel of the Lord—who annihilated the Assyrian troops, forcing Sennacherib to retreat to Assyria with his tail between his legs. One relatively small city relying on an omnipotent God had put to shame a massive army who trusted in false gods. Once again David had defeated Goliath by trusting in God's power.

All this is plain to see in the pages of Scripture. But wait, there's more! What is hidden from most readers of the Bible is the parallel account preserved for us in the words of the Assyrian king himself! Sennacherib has left for us a record of this event, written in the cuneiform Assyrian language, though understandably spun in a way that puts this humiliating defeat in the best possible light. Here is his account, in his own words:

> As for Hezekiah, the Judean, I besieged forty-six of his fortified walled cities and surrounding smaller towns, which were without number. Using packed-down ramps and applying battering rams, infantry attacks by mines, breeches, and siege machines, I conquered (them). I took out 200,150 people, young and old, male and female, horses, mules, donkeys, camels, cattle, and sheep, without number, and counted them as spoil. He himself, I locked up within Jerusalem, his royal city, like a bird in a cage. I surrounded him with earthworks, and made it unthinkable for him to exit by the city gate.[2]

Taken on its own, this record reads like quite a victory for Sennacherib. But when this section of his annals is read in its larger context, an important difference becomes apparent. When he recounts his victories over other kings in this military campaign, Sennacherib describes how those kings "bowed in submission at my feet," "kissed my feet," or were "deported and brought to Assyria."[3] We don't find these expressions in Sennacherib's account regarding Hezekiah. The most Sennacherib can say about Hezekiah's fate is that he was confined in the city "like a bird in a cage"—not such a bad outcome for rebellion against the reigning world power! Sennacherib mentions nothing about the catastrophic loss of a hundred and eighty-five thousand of his troops in a single night, nor of his hasty, panicked retreat to the Assyrian capital of Nineveh. Of course, these details would hardly be mentioned on an Assyrian commemorative victory stele!

Another detail recorded in the Bible (2 Kgs 19:37) and corroborated by surviving historical records is that one of Sennacherib's sons assassinated him. After his ignominious departure from Jerusalem, and thinking himself safe in his own city, Sennacherib was murdered by one of his sons, who hoped to succeed him to the throne.[4] In a wonderful irony, it was not Hezekiah who was killed in his capital city, but rather the king who threatened to kill him!

Our passage, therefore, has corroboration from the archives of the very kingdom that threatened God's people. Sennacherib had to begrudgingly admit that yes, in fact, he had not been able to add Hezekiah to his list of defeated kings. And the Assyrian records report Sennacherib's murder inside his capital city—the same fate he desired for Hezekiah. Despite every initial indication to the contrary, the God of Judah demonstrated that he was indeed mightier than the gods of Assyria. That our God is mightier than any threat that may come our way, no matter how gigantic that threat may be, is another truth that is often hidden behind the visible realities that assail his people. But it remains true nonetheless. And that's something even God's enemies are ultimately forced to admit.

THINGS TO CONSIDER

1. The king of Assyria appeared for a while as though he were stronger than God himself. Do any troubles in your life seem stronger than God's ability to deal with them? How might you remind yourself who is ultimately in control?

2. Why do you think God sometimes allows his own people to be confronted with circumstances or antagonists that seem to overwhelm them? Did it appear that circumstances or antagonists had overwhelmed Jesus? Reflect on how God might use these situations to advance his own redemptive purposes.

3. In the face of a great threat to his nation, King Ahaz turned away from his faith in the Lord to faith in the king of Assyria. And even King Hezekiah was willing to compromise his faith to avoid grave danger. Have you compromised your faith for a similar reason? Can you imagine any situation that would lead you to do so?

13

—o—

UNFINISHED BUSINESS

King Xerxes honored Haman son
of Hammedatha, the Agagite.
—ESTHER 3:1

When we read through the historical narratives of the Bible, we may find ourselves quickly skimming over some details that we judge to be relatively superfluous. We may be tempted to regard these details in the same way we regard those provided by some of our relatives whose stories of times past are so festooned with the minutiae of when the events took place (Was it in late spring or early summer?) or who was there (Was it the son of Uncle Ralph's friend or was it his grandson?) that we find ourselves growing impatient and our brains beginning to cramp up. "Just give me the main points and let's move on!" we may think (to ourselves of course). But the Bible is not like our chatty Aunt Tillie. The details it provides have significance and add depth to its narratives, even if they aren't immediately apparent to us who are so far removed from the times and places involved that we no longer notice what would have been obvious to the original audience. However much these details of the biblical accounts may seem to be a distraction to us, they are divinely inspired and so also deserve our careful attention. In our passage, we will give that careful attention to one of these surprisingly significant details.

Esther 3:1 introduces us to a key figure in the story, "Haman son of Hammedatha, the Agagite." Haman's father, Hammedatha, is unknown to us apart from repeated references to him in the book of Esther (3:1, 10; 8:5; 9:10, 24), where, unfortunately, we aren't told anything else about him. Hammedatha is a Persian name, but its precise meaning is unclear.[1] The repetition of this Persian name throughout the book is at least a further reminder that God's people are in exile, dominated by a foreign power. But the force and threat of this foreign power come to a focus in Hammedatha's son, Haman. His importance in the narrative is underscored by the fact that his name appears forty-nine times in the book (fifty-four in Hebrew), about the same frequency as the names of the two representatives on the other side of the power struggle, Mordecai and Esther.[2] But it is the additional detail added to Haman's name that would have caught the attention of every Israelite who heard it and so deserves some deeper consideration from us as well. Haman was an *Agagite*!

The mention of Agag, a historical king of the Amalekites, would immediately remind the original readers and hearers of the failings of their first king, Saul, recounted in 1 Samuel 15. We're told in that biblical account that the Lord had determined to "punish the Amalekites for what they did to Israel when they waylaid them as they came up from Egypt" (15:2). So the Lord commanded Saul to attack them, destroy all their property, and put to death every last one of them (15:3). Although Saul did attack the Amalekites, he "spared Agag [their king][3] and the best of the sheep and cattle, the fat calves and lambs—everything that was good" (15:9). Through his prophet Samuel, God rebuked Saul for his disobedience and rejected him as king over his people: "Because you have rejected the word of the LORD, he has rejected you as king" (15:23).

And now, in the book of Esther, Saul's unfinished business has led to a situation where God's people are imperiled. Haman, a descendant of the Amalekite king Agag, was in a position to carry out his intent to destroy all the Jews throughout the whole Persian Empire (Esth 3:7)! If only Saul had been obedient to the Lord! If he had, this entire situation could conceivably have been avoided. Haman the Agagite might never have been born, and this threat to the Jews wouldn't exist.

But Haman had indeed been born, and the Jews would find themselves in dire straits because of him. The only hope the Jews would have for deliverance from Haman's targeted malevolence seemed to rest with two unlikely characters in the story, the cousins Esther and Mordecai. Esther had been involuntarily taken to the Persian king's palace to become a member of his harem (2:8). Her subsequent power as Xerxes's queen could hardly be more than Vashti's, who had been summarily deposed. Surely the fate of the previous queen weighed heavily on Esther's mind. Moreover, Mordecai would fall into Haman's disfavor by refusing to bow down to him (3:2–4), the very reason for Haman's relentless drive to exterminate all the Jews.

The power mismatch as the story progresses seems to be

overwhelming. On one side were two Jewish captives (although Esther had hidden her Jewish ethnicity). On the other side was a Persian official who occupied "a seat of honor higher than that of all the other nobles" (3:1). Even though Esther was queen, she could have no influence on the king unless he allowed her into his presence. But, as we're later told, she would not be summoned for thirty days and risked death by seeking an audience with him unbidden (4:11). In the face of this bleak reality, there did not seem to be much hope for the Jews' deliverance. Nevertheless, through a combination of Mordecai's insightfulness, Esther's bravery, and the providential care of a loving and faithful God, the crisis was miraculously averted. (For examples of God's providence in this narrative, see no. 3 under Things to Consider.) Not only did Haman's plot fail, it failed spectacularly! He was executed in precisely the same way he had planned to have Mordecai executed, on the pole Haman himself had set up for Mordecai (7:9–10). Instead of the Jews being plundered and killed by their enemies, the Jews were granted the right by royal decree to plunder and kill *them* (8:11). Mordecai and Esther were honored, while Haman and his sons were executed (9:7–10).

But wait, there's more! The narrator provides yet another detail that further deepens our appreciation for what God is doing in this historical account. Early in the story, the narrator inserts a detail regarding Mordecai that is found only in a single verse in the entire book: Mordecai came from the tribe of Benjamin (2:5), and because Esther was his cousin (2:7), she was a Benjaminite as well. Is this an irrelevant detail à la Aunt Tillie? Hardly. This detail calls readers back once again to the tragic disobedience of King Saul, who was also from the tribe of Benjamin, and highlights the striking turnaround God is accomplishing through Mordecai and Esther: A Benjaminite king (Saul) lost his power because of the faithlessness he demonstrated when confronted with Agag; the Benjaminite captives (Mordecai and Esther) gained their power because of the faithfulness they demonstrated when confronted by the Agagite Haman.[4]

It had taken a long time for God to bring about this reversal. The Benjaminite Saul revealed his faithlessness regarding Agag sometime in the second half of the eleventh century BC. The Benjaminites Mordecai and Esther revealed their faithfulness regarding the Agagite Haman sometime in the first half of the fifth century BC—a span of about 550 years! God had determined to destroy the Amalekites (1 Sam 15:2), but the last Amalekite representative recorded in the Bible—Haman—had determined instead to destroy the Jews. Needless to say, God won that contest, even though the realization of that victory took a long time.

Similarly, God has determined to conquer sin and all its negative effects. He accomplished this by sending another unlikely hero: a baby, born to a carpenter, who would grow to be one who would sacrifice himself for the ultimate salvation of all his people. Just as it didn't look like Mordecai and Esther could possibly save God's people in the face of the magnitude of evil arrayed against them, so it didn't look like Jesus could possibly save God's people in the face of the magnitude of evil arrayed against him. But God's power at work behind the scenes guaranteed the victory of Mordecai and Esther over Haman the Agagite. And God's power at work through the life, death, and resurrection of Jesus—who is uncoincidentally described in Balaam's prophecy as a king greater than Agag (Num 24:7)—guarantees the victory of his people over sin and death (1 Cor 15:54–57).

This is a sure outcome for all who put their faith in Jesus, no matter how great the power imbalance may seem at the present time (1 John 5:4, 5). However, as in the case of the ultimate eradication of the Amalekites, the ultimate eradication of sin and its effects may take some time.

We have discovered a surprising significance for two seemingly irrelevant details in the book of Esther—that Haman was an Agagite and that Mordecai and Esther were Benjaminites. These details link this story to the unfinished business that resulted from the disobedience of Saul, Israel's first king. Reflecting on that connection has opened for us a whole other depth of meaning for this well-known story and prophetically pointed us toward the analogous situation in the New Testament that finds its expression in the last and greatest king of God's people, Jesus Christ. For reasons known only to him, God may take some time to accomplish his stated purposes, but that accomplishment is no less certain, a fact Haman found out the hard way.

THINGS TO CONSIDER

1. Saul's unfinished business, his disobedience to God, resulted not only in harm to himself but ultimately in a threat to the continued existence of the Jewish people. In your own efforts to obey God, are there any areas of unfinished business?

2. Going along with the crowd sometimes seems like the best course of action. If Mordecai had bowed down to Haman along with everyone else, he would not have

stirred up Haman's wrath. If Esther had followed custom and rejected Mordecai's instructions to enter the king's presence without being summoned, her life would not have been placed in jeopardy. Are you experiencing pressure from the crowd to "go along to get along"? What do you risk if you go with the crowd? What do you risk if you don't?

3. Although God is not explicitly mentioned in the book of Esther, his providential activity is obvious in Mordecai overhearing the plot on the king's life, in Esther being in a position to make an appeal to the king, in the king's insomnia leading to his reading the account of Mordecai's actions on his behalf, and in many other ways as well. Can you point to a situation in your life where you became aware of God's providential activity on your behalf?

14

—o—

THE CLOUD RIDER

Extol him who rides on the clouds.
—Psalm 68:4

In Psalm 68:4, we may understand the description of God as one "who rides on the clouds" to be simply a creative way of describing God in his heavenly abode. The language may call to mind paintings (such as that of the Italian Renaissance painter Raphael in his *Madonna of San Sisto* or that of Michelangelo in his *Creation of Adam*) that depict corpulent cherubs in the downy clouds of heaven, often playing harps as they flit to and fro on tiny wings in the presence of God. But an examination of texts found not so long ago from a culture in a position to influence Israel reveals a much deeper meaning for our verse. We pause, therefore, to consider the culture of Ugarit.

Unless you are a history buff with a particular interest and emphasis on ancient lands, you most likely have never heard of

Ugarit. It's not even mentioned anywhere in the Bible. But Ugarit was an important and influential city-state whose origins extend back in time to before Israel became a nation. The earliest surviving letter from an Ugaritic king is that of Ammištamru I, who reigned before 1370 BC.[1] Depending on one's chronology, this is about the time Israel was engaged in the conquest of the promised land. Ugarit was located on the coast of the Mediterranean Sea only a couple of hundred miles from what would be the northern border of Israel. Its influence in the region was multiplied because of where it was situated. Ugarit had a prime location at the intersection of the east-west trade route, extending from the Mediterranean Sea to the heartland of the ancient Near East, and the north-south trade route, extending from Egypt in the south to Hatti and Mitanni in the north. Ugarit passed out of existence about a hundred and fifty years before Israel became a monarchy under Saul, its first king. A library of documents subsequently discovered at the ruins of Ugarit in 1929 has opened a window into the mythology of the region that Israel encountered from the time of the conquest to the time of the judges.

We need to look through that window into the broader world that the Ugaritic texts reveal so that we avoid the pitfall of reading the Bible with a kind of cultural myopia. This affliction is characterized by reading the biblical texts as though Israel were the only nation that existed on the face of the earth. Our gaze can be so focused on Israel that we fail to notice in our peripheral vision the surrounding cultures that may have exerted significant pressures on the people of God, for good or ill. It is just as negligent and irresponsible to ignore Ugarit's influence on those who lived in Canaan as it would be, for example, to ignore the tremendous influence Mexico and other nations to the south have had on the southwest region of the US in the areas of language, food, art, architecture, beliefs, and values.

If we want to avoid such cultural myopia and be able to understand the deeper meaning of our seemingly ordinary verse, therefore, we need to give some attention to this northern neighbor of Israel, the city-state of Ugarit, and particularly to the mythology it presents in its ancient texts. Because when we do, we'll immediately encounter there a prominent figure familiar to all readers of the Old Testament, the god Baal.

The word *baʿal* is a common Semitic noun meaning "lord" or "owner," but it also appears in ancient Near Eastern texts as the proper name of an important and powerful god. In Ugaritic mythology, Baal was the principal actor and chief deity, a position he earned through combat with (and ultimate victory over) rival gods. His elevated status in the divine pantheon is reflected in his frequent designation as "the prince, the lord/master of the earth" (*zabūlu baʿlu ʾarṣi*).[2] Most important for understanding our verse is the fact that he was also identified as the god of the storm. He was therefore associated with all the natural phenomena associated with storms: clouds, thunder, lightning, and rain.[3] Consider, for example, a couple of passages from the Ugaritic Baal epic:

> Baʿlu can send his rain in due season,
>> send the season of driving showers;
> (can) Baʿlu shout aloud in the clouds,
>> shoot (his) lightning-bolts to the earth.[4]

> Baʿlu . . . opens up the rift in the clouds,
>> Baʿlu emits his holy voice,

Ba'lu makes the thunder roll over and
over again.
His [holy] voice [causes] the earth [to tremble],
[at his thunder] the mountains shake
with fear.[5]

This picturesque imagery reveals that the clouds associated with Baal (or Ba'lu) are among the many manifestations of Baal's fearsome presence. He was believed to be the god of the storm, so the clouds on which he is pictured as riding should not be thought of as the fluffy cumulus clouds that float along languidly in the azure summer sky. Instead, they should be thought of as the ominous cumulonimbus clouds that herald the coming of a powerful storm. In fact, they should be regarded as his war chariot, on which he rides forth to manifest his power. That is why in the Baal epic, the epithet "Mighty Baal" is often paralleled with "Cloud Rider"[6]—the same expression used to describe God in Psalm 68:4! The parallel is even more obvious when the relevant terms in the languages of both cultures are rendered in English letters. In the Ugaritic language of the Baal epic, "Cloud Rider" is *rkb 'rpt*; in the Hebrew language of Psalm 68:4, "him who rides on the clouds" is *rkb . . . 'rbt*. These are virtually identical expressions. The only difference is a *p* in the Ugaritic where there is a *b* in the Hebrew; but this difference is negligible because the interchange between these two consonants occurs quite frequently in the Semitic language family,[7] to which both Ugaritic and Hebrew belong.

This, of course, raises the question of why an expression used to describe a Canaanite deity is used in the Bible to describe God.

The answer to this question reveals the hidden depth of meaning in this biblical verse. King David and his ancient audience were no doubt quite aware of the well-known description of Baal as "Cloud Rider." It is precisely their awareness that gives this verse its punch. David is not only asserting that God is the one who comes in cloud and storm to blow his enemies away like smoke (68:2) and causes those who trust in him to be glad and rejoice (68:3), he is also asserting that God is the *only* one who can do these things, despite what any of the surrounding nations may think. He alone is the God of the storm.

About three thousand years later, the Son of God would powerfully demonstrate the same point to his terrified disciples during a furious storm on the Sea of Galilee when he rebuked the winds and the waves, restoring perfect calm (Matt 8:23–27). They rightly conclude, "Even the winds and the waves obey him!" Our deeper understanding of Psalm 68:4 would cause us to place the accent on the last word of Matthew 8:27: "Even the winds and the waves obey *him* [and not Baal]!" That all authority in heaven and on earth belongs to God alone is affirmed again by the Son of God after his resurrection (Matt 28:18).

As with the Cloud Rider of Ugaritic mythology, the one who rides on the clouds in the biblical texts comes in the storm to both judge and bless. These two aspects of God's stormy presence are found in the three verses that come immediately before Psalm 68:4. The New Testament describes the same stormy coming of the Son of God "on the clouds of heaven" to judge the living and the dead at the end of the age (Matt 24:30; 26:64; Mark 13:26; 14:62; Luke 21:27). At that time there will be no more doubt in anyone's mind about who is truly in control of all aspects of creation. As powerful as a storm can be, there is one (and only one) who is even more powerful. May we be among those looking forward to his coming and not fearing it.

THINGS TO CONSIDER

1. When Christians engage with the culture, we must always decide what things from the culture align with our faith, what things must be rejected as contradictory to our faith, and what things can be accepted with modification. In Psalm 68:4, David accepted with (major) modification a description of a deity from Ugaritic mythology. What are some beliefs or practices from the surrounding culture that you believe a Christian can accept with modification? What things must be rejected? How do you deal with Christians who disagree with you about your decisions?

2. In Ugaritic mythology, Baal was credited as the source of natural phenomena such as thunder, lightning, and rain. Who or what do people credit as the source of these phenomena today? Fate? Chance? Mother Nature? What expressions used to describe these sources could you modify to appropriately apply to God?

3. If the Son of God returned today accompanied by powerful meteorological phenomena, would you be happy to see him? Or terrified? Why might that be?

15

—o—

HERE THERE BE
DRAGONS

It was you who split open the sea by your power;
you broke the heads of the monster in
the waters.
It was you who crushed the heads of Leviathan.
—PSALM 74:13-14

The Latin *hic sunt dracones* ("here there be dragons") was
a warning written on ancient maps to indicate those areas
that were unexplored or considered dangerous because of the
suspected presence there of dragons, sea monsters, or other
terrors of the deep. Although unlikely to be adopted by any contemporary Bible translation, this Latin warning would be an
appropriate heading for Psalm 74:13-14 because, it may surprise

you to learn, there indeed be dragons lurking in the depths of this passage, and their presence there has surprising significance.

The first evidence of such a monster lies hidden just below the surface of the English word "sea." One might expect there is something more to be understood about this entity because of the descriptions the psalmist provides for it in the rest of this passage, things difficult to conceptualize if the word simply referred to the physical sea. The English word "sea" is a perfectly fine translation of the Hebrew word *yām* (יָם) used in this passage. But this word would have had an additional depth of meaning to those who heard it, especially in the context of 74:13–14. In the mythology of Ugarit, the close geographical and chronological neighbor of Israel (described in the previous chapter), Yam (the Ugaritic equivalent of the Hebrew word *yām*) challenges Baal for supremacy but is ultimately defeated by him. And so Baal earns for himself supremacy among the gods and the right to a temple. In the same Ugaritic mythological texts, we find descriptions of Yam. He is called "Lôtan [*ltn*], the fleeing serpent, . . . the twisting serpent, the close-coiling one with seven heads."[1] In yet another passage, Baal describes Yam as a dragon that he has vanquished: "I have bound the dragon's [*tnn*] jaws, [I] have destroyed it."[2] All of these designations are important because they all find parallels in biblical texts. And many of those parallels are found in Ps 74:13–14.

In the Hebrew text of our passage, in addition to the allusion to Yam we have already observed in verse 13, we also find an allusion to his other Ugaritic name, Lôtan. The Ugaritic writing system employs only consonants, so the name Lôtan appears in Ugaritic texts as *ltn*. In the Hebrew text of 74:14, these same consonants reappear in the word לִוְיָתָן (*liwyātān*), commonly rendered in English translations as "Leviathan."

There is yet one more allusion to Yam in our passage. In verse 13 he is referred to as a multiple-headed monster in the waters. We have already seen in the previously cited Ugaritic mythological text that Yam or Lôtan is described as having seven heads. We would be justified, therefore, in suspecting that the multiple-headed monster of the biblical text and the seven-headed monster of the Ugaritic text refer to the same creature. That the term translated as "monster" in our passage indeed refers to Yam is confirmed by the agreement between the Hebrew and Ugaritic words used to describe it. In the Ugaritic text, Baal describes Yam as the "dragon" he has defeated. In the Ugaritic text, this word is written *tnn*. In the Hebrew text of 74:13, the word translated as "monster" is תַּנִּין. Rendering this word in English letters results in *tannîn*. Again, because the Ugaritic language writes only the consonants, it would render this Hebrew word as *t-nn-n*. Moreover, Ugaritic does not indicate doubled consonants. So it would render *t-nn-n* as *t-n-n*—exactly the same letters it uses in its own text to describe Yam!

What is going on here? Why is this mythological beast with divine status, from a non-Israelite culture, allowed to romp around in the sacred texts of Israel? Is the historical concept of monotheism in jeopardy? To answer these critically important questions, we first need to examine the broader context of our passage and also investigate how these mythological terms are used in the rest of the Old Testament.

Psalm 74 is a lament psalm. Common in biblical laments is reflection on God's saving works of the past in order to bolster confidence that he will act the same way in whatever current crisis the psalmist is facing. In Psalm 74, this reflection begins in verse 12—the exact center of the psalm—which comes immediately before our passage. In this verse, the psalmist asserts his belief that just as God has brought salvation in the past, he will certainly continue to be a saving God in the future. In the very next verse, the first verse of our passage, the psalmist reflects on one of those divine acts of salvation, one that involved God exerting his power over the sea. The signature saving event that involved God and the sea is surely the crossing of the Red Sea in Israel's exodus from Egypt.

So it appears that the psalmist is conscripting imagery from Ugaritic mythological literature to symbolically communicate God's victory over Egypt at the Red Sea. Other biblical texts support this conclusion. In Ezekiel 29:3, for example, the Lord says, "I am against you, Pharaoh king of Egypt, you great monster lying among your streams." Another example occurs a few chapters later, where Ezekiel is commanded to "take up a lament concerning Pharaoh king of Egypt and say to him: 'You are like a lion among the nations; you are like a monster in the seas'" (32:2). In both of these verses, the pharaoh of Egypt is described as a monster. The Hebrew word used in both cases is *tannîn*[3]— the same word found in our passage as a designation of Yam.

But Egypt is not the only enemy of God and his people to be depicted this way in the biblical texts. In Isaiah 27:1, for example, we read about a day when God will vanquish all his enemies. The language the prophet uses incorporates many of the terms for Yam we have already discussed (indicated in italics):

In that day,

the Lord will punish with his sword—
his fierce, great and powerful sword—

> *Leviathan the gliding serpent,*
> *Leviathan the coiling serpent;*
> he will slay the *monster* of the sea.

This imagery extends even to the New Testament, where Revelation 12:3, for example, describes the final battle between God and "an enormous red dragon with seven heads" to refer to God's ultimate victory over the forces of evil arrayed against him and his people. The Greek word translated as "dragon" in this verse is δρακων (*drakōn*). This is the word the Septuagint (the Greek translation of the Old Testament) consistently uses to translate the word *tannîn*, which we recognize from the Ugaritic mythological texts as referring to the seven-headed dragon.

Our investigation of the immediate and broader biblical context of Psalm 74:13–14 has revealed that the biblical writers frequently used images from Ugaritic mythological literature to communicate biblical truth, particularly regarding God's saving activity. It is important to note, however, that in every biblical occurrence, the imagery is precisely that—*imagery* and not *reality*. Yam (or his other designations) is never depicted as equal to God or even as a serious threat. Yet the question remains: Why was this imagery used? There are at least two reasons.

The first reason has to do with convenience. Because this imagery was well known, it communicated easily and powerfully the message the biblical writers wished to convey. It would be like someone today saying to a person who just demonstrated an amazing athletic feat, "You're Superman!" Or referring to a person with a destructive temper as Godzilla. In both cases, the reality of these mythological beings is not being proposed.

Rather, these images are evoked as a convenient way to communicate a powerful idea in only a few words.

The second reason has to do with the appropriateness of the imagery itself. In the Ugaritic mythological literature, Yam challenged Baal's claim to supremacy among the gods. Therefore, when the biblical writers refer to Egypt or any other worldly power as Yam (or one of his other designations), they are indicating by this mythological terminology that the earthly power is illegitimately and foolishly challenging God's right to supremacy. And just as Baal vanquished Yam, so God will ultimately vanquish all who oppose him, because the Savior, Jesus Christ, is seated at the right hand of God, "far above all rule and authority, power and dominion, and every name that is invoked, not only in the present age but also in the one to come" (Eph 1:21). All these things can be concisely and powerfully communicated by simply referring to any of God's foes as Yam—a terrifying threat whose demise is nevertheless certain. In the words of Jesus, "In this world you will have trouble. But take heart! I have overcome the world" (John 16:33). There indeed be dragons in this world, but Jesus has overcome them and is in the process of eradicating them.

THINGS TO CONSIDER

1. In our passage (and, as we have seen, other biblical texts as well), Yam was used as a shorthand and metaphorical term to refer to real and present challenges to the authority of God and the well-being of his people. From your perspective, what things in your life or in the life of God's church could be called Yam today?

2. The psalmist used words drawn from Ugaritic mythology to give his readers and hearers a mental picture of God's power, supremacy, and certain victory over the forces of evil. That conceptual framework is understandably lost on most readers of the English Bible today because of their unfamiliarity with Ugaritic culture. What imagery from contemporary culture would you use to communicate the same idea?

3. The end of every enemy of God and his people is coming. Until then, however, the church continues to be under attack. In Revelation 12:9, the architect of these attacks is described in terms once again drawn from Ugaritic mythology: "the great dragon . . . that ancient serpent called the devil, or Satan, who leads the whole world astray." What resources for spiritual warfare are available to God's people until their enemies are eradicated?

16

—o—

STREET SMARTS

For giving prudence to those who are simple . . .
—PROVERBS 1:4

At first glance, apart from the use of some words not encountered very often in contemporary conversation, there doesn't seem to be anything surprisingly significant about Proverbs 1:4, sitting innocuously near the beginning of the book. But when we lift up the lid and look underneath, we might be surprised to discover a depth of meaning that likely escaped our notice. When we consider the Hebrew underlying our English translations, we can understand more fully the intended benefit of these proverbs for our physical and spiritual lives. And certainly surprisingly, and perhaps even shockingly, that benefit is associated with the Bible's most abhorrent and malevolent character.

The book of Proverbs, as we're informed in the opening verses, was written to provide a whole array of benefits to those who are willing to internalize its wisdom. Even before we arrive at our verse, we are told that the proverbs contained in this book will enable us to gain wisdom and instruction, understand words of insight (1:2), and receive instruction in prudent behavior so that we can do what is right and just and fair (1:3). The list of benefits continues with our verse, in which we are told these proverbs will also give *prudence* to those who are *simple*. We recognize that "simple" is not an adjective most people would like to have ascribed to them. So those with even a modicum of self-esteem might conclude that this book was not written for them. After all, they might rationalize, *they* aren't simple and so they don't need the proffered prudence, thank you very much! But this conclusion would be based on a faulty understanding of the biblical meaning of the word "simple."

Unlike its frequent use in our contemporary culture to refer to those who are simple-minded, uncultured, or those for whom we might say the elevator doesn't go all the way to the top floor, the Hebrew word translated as "simple" here does not have anything at all to do with mental acuity or even urbane sophistication. It refers instead to those who are inexperienced or untrained in the potentially dangerous ways of the world and human beings. Such people are overly trusting, naive, easily led astray. They are blissfully unaware of the self-serving calculations and machinations of those intending to do them harm. They have not yet grown to any great degree in the hard-earned wisdom that comes from being burned or taken advantage of by others.[1] Unfortunately, this describes all of us at some stage or in some areas of our lives.

None of us is born with immunity from the insidious wiles of those who seek to benefit themselves at our expense. Even age does not always translate into safety from the unscrupulous if the years have not included appropriate life experience. And the most vulnerable among us are those who believe "everyone is basically good at heart," that no one would be heartless enough to intentionally lead them astray. Their confidence in their own perceptiveness or belief in the essential goodness of others is no protection from evil people waiting to ensnare them. However, those who are simple—that is, those who are aware of and admit their vulnerability—have one characteristic that differentiates them from those described in Proverbs as "fools": the simple are teachable. To all of us who are teachable, then, who acknowledge that we too are susceptible to the trickery of malicious opportunists, our verse offers "prudence." But this word in our passage has a surprisingly significant meaning that is probably much deeper than you think it is.

The word "prudence" may not arise frequently (if ever) in our everyday conversation and, if it suggests anything at all, might conjure up images of prim Victorian conservatism or a personality trait usually associated with old-time librarians or schoolmarms (apologies to librarians and schoolmarms everywhere). But in the context of the opening verses of Proverbs, this word is used in a way that suggests an entirely different meaning. Indeed, prudence is presented as the antidote to simpleness. If the simple are those who are easily led astray and taken advantage of, then prudence is something that can prevent that from happening. In contemporary language, we might even describe prudence as "street smarts." Prudence enables us to have our eyes open to the booby traps that have been laid all around us—traps deliberately set for us by those with evil intent and even traps that, like quicksand, occur naturally but are no less dangerous.

The book of Proverbs, therefore, is offering us nothing less than the means to develop an awareness of how things really work in everyday life—the good, the bad, and the ugly—and how to live circumspectly in light of that knowledge. This knowledge is, however, amoral in itself. Its morality depends on how it is used. Consequently, the insight Proverbs gives us into the inner workings of the world and human beings can be used either for good or for evil. But wait, there's more! Through our deeper consideration of this helpful introduction to the ways of the world and the ways of human beings—this prudence, or street smarts—we also discover a hidden and surprising connection between our verse and the very first appearance of evil in the world.

To understand this connection, we have to note some details of the Hebrew underlying our English translations. In 1:4, the pivotal word "prudence" is a translation of the Hebrew word עָרְמָה ('ormâ). In Hebrew, as in all Semitic languages, words are formed around a base of three consonants. By adjusting the vowels, prefixes, and suffixes around these three consonants, different nuances of the word can be expressed. For example, the three consonants ע-מ-ד ('-m-d) always have something to do with standing. Thus, עֲמֹד ('ămōd) means "to stand"; עָמַד ('āmad) means "he stood"; עֹמֵד ('ōmēd) means "standing"; etc. In the case of the word translated as "prudence" in 1:4, the three Hebrew consonants that communicate the basic meaning of the word are ע-ר-ם ('-r-m). The vowels surrounding these consonants let us know that this word עָרְמָה ('ormâ) is a noun. By putting different vowels around these same three consonants, one can express the basic meaning of the word as an adjective. This is precisely what we find in Genesis 3:1, where the serpent in the garden of Eden is described as "more crafty [עָרוּם 'ārûm] than any of the wild animals the LORD God had made." You probably noticed that exactly the same three consonants are used in Genesis 3:1 and Proverbs 1:4: ע-ר-ם ('- r-m). The only difference is that the vowels used to indicate the noun form of the word (Prov 1:4) are different from the vowels used to indicate the adjectival form of the word (Gen 3:1).

At this point we may begin to shrink back from the possible implications of this correspondence. Is Genesis 3:1 calling the serpent *prudent*? Is Proverbs 1:4 encouraging us to be like the serpent in the garden of Eden? Not exactly. Genesis 3:1 is communicating the fact that the serpent had the same street smarts that the book of Proverbs offers its readers. The serpent, however, used that insight for evil instead of good—that is, the serpent knew how human beings think and behave, and it used that knowledge for its own evil purposes. The book of Proverbs, on the other hand, wants its readers to use that knowledge for good purposes. "Prudence" or "shrewdness," therefore, is neither a positive nor a negative characteristic when considered by itself. It's how that situational and interpersonal awareness is used that makes it positive or negative. The serpent used it to deceive the first human beings and lead them into sin. The author of Proverbs intends for human beings to use it to guard against such evil schemes and to navigate safely past them so that their lives can be as successful as possible.

This reexamination of a seemingly ordinary verse helps us understand what Jesus meant when he gave instructions to his twelve disciples before he sent them out with the gospel. He told them that, as they encountered those who would test them mentally and physically, they should "be as shrewd as snakes and as innocent as doves" (Matt 10:16). With our freshly polished understanding of Proverbs 1:4, we could paraphrase this command as follows:

> Use the street smarts that characterized the serpent in the garden of Eden to be aware of how people will try to take advantage of you and turn your words and your circumstances against you. Then you will be able to avoid their malevolent schemes. But as you do so, be as innocent as doves, not using your awareness to become like them by taking advantage of other people for evil purposes of your own!

That we're correct in seeing a connection between Jesus's encouragement to be "as shrewd as snakes" and the shrewdness of the serpent in Genesis 3:1 is supported by the Greek word Jesus used. In the Septuagint (the Greek translation of the Old Testament), the word used to describe the serpent is φρονιμος (*phronimos*). This is exactly the same Greek word Jesus used in Matthew 10:16!

Jesus's words remind the twelve apostles and us that being his disciples does not mean closing our eyes to the realities of life around us. In fact, it means just the opposite. It means being keenly aware of those realities and using that awareness as one more tool to advance the gospel of peace. Christian prudence is an ability to recognize and artfully sidestep the many traps set before us so that we can progress safely along the path of true life and invite others to join us on that path.

What a wonderful depth of meaning has lain hidden in the words of this passage! It only took a little dusting to reveal the beautiful complexity of this seemingly ordinary verse. Our fresh insight into the meaning of these words helps us live out our Christian lives in a world full of "many dangers, toils, and snares,"[2] which we can avoid with a little prudence, available in the book of Proverbs to all those who are ready to be instructed.

THINGS TO CONSIDER

1. Have others taken advantage of you in the past? What advice would you give to someone so that they could avoid being taken advantage of in the same way? Your answer to this question will be your own proverb!

2. Knowing that the Hebrew words in Genesis 3:1 and Proverbs 1:4 are different forms of the same word, how would you translate these two verses so that this hidden connection is more obvious?

3. Do you associate naivete or guilelessness with goodness? If so, does Jesus's command to "be as shrewd as snakes" make you uncomfortable? Can a person have street smarts and retain their innocence at the same time?

17

— o —

WE'VE GOT YOUR NUMBER

The proverbs of Solomon . . .
—PROVERBS 10:1

Those of us who drive the same route to work and home every day can practically do it in our sleep. Many of us have even had the unsettling experience of arriving at home at the end of a busy day and finding ourselves unable to recall any details of our trip! We surely obeyed all the traffic laws, signs, and signals, but the drive was so routine and automatic that we remember nothing about it. Unfortunately, something similar may happen to us when we read over Proverbs 10:1. We are so familiar with the book of Proverbs and with the fact that Solomon authored many proverbs (1 Kgs 4:29–32) that we drive right over this verse and remember nothing about it. But if we give ourselves a couple of (figurative) slaps to rouse ourselves from our stupor, we'll find that there is indeed a deeper meaning here in this seemingly ordinary verse. So let's take in the details of the biblical neighborhood we've driven into and see what there is to find.

The first four words of Proverbs 10:1 (only two in Hebrew: מִשְׁלֵי שְׁלֹמֹה) serve as the title for the section of Proverbs that begins here and ends at 22:16. It's important to note that a different section begins at 22:17 because of the reference in its opening verse to a larger group of people (the wise) than just Solomon alone: "Pay attention and turn your ear to the sayings of the wise." These sayings are later specified as "thirty sayings" (22:20) which we will explore in the following chapter of this book. The significance of the first four words of the section of Proverbs beginning in 10:1 ("the proverbs of Solomon") that we'll be considering here can be fully appreciated only when two often overlooked factors are considered. The first of these is the art of rhetoric. Rhetoric has been described as the "skill in or faculty of using eloquent or persuasive language."[1] As we saw in the previous chapter, the goal of the book of Proverbs is to persuade the reader toward "gaining wisdom and instruction" (1:2), and it uses rhetorical devices to accomplish this end; that is, the book of Proverbs communicates the wisdom it offers not only by means of its content but also by means of its form. *How* it says what it does is just as important as *what* it says. In our efforts to derive the maximum benefit from this book, therefore, we are warranted in looking beyond the words themselves to the way those words are communicated.

The second factor we need to consider is a feature of the Hebrew alphabet of which some might be unaware. Hebrew has no separate characters that it uses for numbers, such as the

Arabic numerals used in English. In Hebrew, the letters of the alphabet are also used to indicate numbers. For example, the first letter of the alphabet (א) is also used for the number 1, the second letter (ב) is used for the number 2, etc. After the ninth letter (ט), every letter counts as a multiple of ten. For example, the tenth letter (י) is used for the number 10, the eleventh letter (כ) is used for the number 20, etc. After the nineteenth letter (צ, used for the number 90), every letter counts as multiple of 100. So the twentieth letter (ק) is used for 100, the twenty-first letter (ר) is used for 200, etc. The Hebrew alphabet and its numerical values are provided on the following chart:

HEBREW LETTER	NUMERICAL VALUE	HEBREW LETTER	NUMERICAL VALUE	HEBREW LETTER	NUMERICAL VALUE
א	1	י	10	ק	100
ב	2	כ	20	ר	200
ג	3	ל	30	ש	300
ד	4	מ	40	ת	400
ה	5	נ	50	ך	500
ו	6	ס	60	ם	600
ז	7	ע	70	ן	700
ח	8	פ	80	ף	800
ט	9	צ	90	ץ	900

Finding the numerical value of a Hebrew word is simply a matter of finding the numerical value of each letter and adding them together. Combining the fact that Hebrew letters have numerical value and the fact that Proverbs uses rhetoric to persuade the reader toward "gaining wisdom and instruction" (1:2) leads us to the deeper meaning in our seemingly ordinary verse. In fact, this rhetorical use of numbers to convey meaning is ancient and is called gematria. So let's look again at our verse from this alphanumeric-rhetorical perspective; that is, by using gematria.

Clearly, the most significant word in our verse is the name Solomon, the wise man par excellence (1 Kgs 4:29–34). If there was ever going to be additional meaning in someone's name, it would be in this man's! In Hebrew, Solomon's name is שלמה. Using the previous chart, we can determine its numerical value:

$$
\begin{array}{rl}
\text{ש} = & 300 \\
\text{ל} = & 30 \\
\text{מ} = & 40 \\
\text{ה} = & \underline{5} \\
& 375
\end{array}
$$

Gematria is usually understood to refer to the symbolic meaning that numbers have in themselves.[2] But in our examination of Prov 10:1, we will take the much less exegetically risky path of simply looking for some correspondence between the numerical value of Solomon's name and something in the biblical text with the same value. An example of such intentional correspondence is provided for us in an extrabiblical inscription from the Neo-Assyrian king Sargon II, dated to the eighth century BC. In it, Sargon says, "16,283 cubits, the numeral of my name, I made the circuit of its [i.e., Khorsabad's] wall."[3] In other words, Sargon intentionally built the wall around Khorsabad so that the measurement of its circumference in cubits would be the same as the numerical value of his name. That leads us to question whether something similar might be true about Solomon. Perhaps, like Sargon, he created something with the same number as the numerical value of his name.

Our first clue that something else, something deeper, is being communicated by the numerical value of Solomon's name (375) lies in the fact that it seems a bit unusual to reintroduce Solomon as the source of these proverbs when he has *already* been introduced as such at the beginning of the book (Prov 1:1), and no one else has been introduced as another author since then. So the intentional repetition of Solomon's name at the beginning of this particular collection of proverbs within the book of Proverbs must be meaningful. To begin to understand that significance, let's look a little closer at the collection itself.

As noted above, this subunit of Proverbs ends at 22:16. So "the proverbs of Solomon" in this case must refer to the collection of proverbs found in 10:1–22:16. This is a large portion of the book of Proverbs. And it is instructive to see exactly how many proverbs this large portion contains. When all the proverbs in this section are added up, the number comes to precisely 375—the exact numerical value of Solomon's name! This correspondence in numbers can hardly be coincidental. So what is the intended rhetorical effect of this phenomenon within this wisdom book? To answer that question, we need to reflect on the meaning of wisdom itself.

Biblical wisdom is based on the fear of the Lord (1:7; 9:10).

It proceeds from an acknowledgment that God has created an orderly world (e.g., natural laws, a moral compass [Rom 2:14–15], an appropriate time for everything [Eccl 3:1–8]). To fear God in the orderly world he has created means we should seek to understand that order and align our lives with it. Because only by doing so will we experience maximum fulfillment as human beings.[4] Living according to the order God placed in the world is characterized by a certain fittingness or appropriateness to our actions; that is, living according to biblical wisdom involves the appropriate behavior, word, response, or initiative for the appropriate time, occasion, context, or person.

And it is no surprise that the inspired wisdom that describes that divine order in the world should itself be orderly as well! How appropriate is it that Solomon, the archetypal wise human being, should utter wisdom sayings whose number is *his* number? By means of the numerical value of his name, we are reminded that the 375 wisdom sayings are identified with Mr. 375. In other words, we are being reminded by means of a clever rhetorical device (gematria) that Solomon = wisdom, and we should therefore listen to what he has to say if we truly desire to "find life and receive favor from the LORD" (8:35). This is the surprising significance of the two Hebrew words that comprise 10:1, a significance that ultimately points us to the fuller revelation of wisdom revealed in the New Testament. For if the book of Proverbs encourages us to listen to Solomon in order to become wise, how much more should we listen to the one who is greater than Solomon (Matt 12:42)—Jesus Christ, "who has become for us wisdom from God" (1 Cor 1:30) and "in whom are hidden all the treasures of wisdom and knowledge" (Col 2:3)?

THINGS TO CONSIDER

1. Is the wisdom described in 10:1–22:16 something that only the people of God can realize? If not, is there a difference between the wisdom of unbelievers and that of believers? If you think there is, can you give an example of each? If the fear of the Lord is the beginning of wisdom, can those who fear the Lord benefit from the wisdom of those who don't?

2. Do you believe there is a difference between wisdom and holiness or sanctification? If so, how would you describe that difference? How does sin interfere with attaining wisdom? How might sin affect our motives, perceptions, or abilities? What resources do we have for growing in wisdom?

3. Reflect on how Jesus is the fulfillment of wisdom. How did he live in a way that reflects divine wisdom? Because Jesus is both human and divine, is it possible for us to live as he did? What do the commands to be wise found in the New Testament (Matt 10:16; Rom 16:19; 1 Cor 3:18; Eph 5:15; Col 4:5) add to our understanding?

18

—o—

Divine Design

Have I not written thirty sayings for you?
—Proverbs 22:20

The mention of "thirty sayings" in Proverbs 22:20 might strike some of us as a bit strange. After all, over twenty-one chapters of wisdom sayings have already been encountered in Proverbs by the time the reader arrives at this verse. So why would this particular group of thirty sayings be singled out for special attention? The thirty sayings found in Prov 22:17–24:22 (indicated in the NIV by helpful, supplied headings throughout these chapters), though instructive, don't seem to be especially significant. And the points that some of these sayings make have already been stated previously, even if not in exactly the same way. For example, 22:26 has already been stated in different words in 11:15; 23:21 in 21:17; 23:27–28 in 5:3–6; 24:1 in 3:31;

etc. And "have I not written" seems to imply that the sayings have already been presented, not that they are yet to come in the following chapters; that is, we would instead expect something like this: "Here are another thirty sayings for you." So why are these sayings being enumerated, when were they written (and by whom), and what is the deeper meaning in these seemingly ordinary verses? It may be surprising to learn that our inquiry into these issues leads to literature outside of the Bible, from a nation that was historically an enemy of Israel.

Most biblical scholars have proposed that answers to the questions we have raised can be found through consideration of another wisdom collection in the ancient Near East that came to light in 1888. This collection, called the Instruction of Amenemope, is attributed to a court official named Amenemope (or Amen-em-Opet), the son of Kanakht. Amenemope is described as "experienced in his office, the offspring of a scribe of Egypt."[1] Several similarities with the "Thirty Sayings of the Wise" in Proverbs make this Egyptian wisdom collection intriguing. The first is that it is also divided into thirty sayings (or chapters). The fact that the biblical reference to "thirty sayings" in our verse and the thirty chapters of the Instruction of Amenemope are the only two wisdom collections that we know of from history that utilize this division into thirty sections strongly suggests some kind of relationship between these two compositions.

The probability of relationship between this section of the book of Proverbs and the Instruction of Amenemope is strengthened further by the fact that in addition to the form, the content of the two wisdom texts also has similarities. Already at the beginning of each wisdom collection (i.e., the introduction to the

Instruction of Amenemope and the opening verses of the biblical "Thirty Sayings of the Wise"), we find a parallel. The Egyptian text states that its purpose is to provide instruction in "knowing how to answer one who speaks, to reply to one who sends a message"[2]—in other words, how to be a trustworthy intermediary. This same purpose is found at the beginning of the biblical "Thirty Sayings of the Wise": "teaching you to be honest and to speak the truth, so that you bring back truthful reports to those you serve" (Prov 22:21).

Other parallels between the two compositions are listed in the following table:

AMENEMOPE	PROVERBS (22:17–24:22)
Give your ears, hear the sayings, give your heart to understand them; it profits to put them in your heart. . . . Let them rest in the casket of your belly. . . . They'll be a mooring post for your tongue. (III:9–16)	Pay attention and turn your ear to the sayings of the wise; apply your heart to what I teach, for it is pleasing when you keep them in your heart and have all of them ready on your lips. (22:17–18)
Beware of robbing a wretch, of attacking a cripple. (IV:4–5)	Do not exploit the poor because they are poor and do not crush the needy in court. (22:22)
Do not move the markers on the borders of fields. (VII:11)	Do not move an ancient boundary stone set up by your ancestors. (22:28)
[Riches] made themselves wings like geese, and flew away to the sky. (X:4–5)	Cast but a glance at riches, and they are gone, for they will surely sprout wings and fly off to the sky like an eagle. (23:5)

AMENEMOPE	PROVERBS (22:17–24:22)
Do not befriend the heated man, nor approach him for conversation. (XI.14)	Do not make friends with a hot-tempered person, do not associate with one easily angered. (22:24)
The scribe who is skilled in his office, he is found worthy to be a courtier. (XXVII:16–17)	Do you see someone skilled in their work? They will serve before kings; they will not serve before officials of low rank. (22:29)[3]

These parallels, when taken together, argue strongly for some degree of relationship between these two texts. The date of the composition of the Instruction of Amenemope is difficult to determine with certainty, but scholars agree that it most probably falls in the Ramesside period (1292–1069 BC).[4] Proverbs 25:1 tells us that at least some of Solomon's proverbs were "compiled by the men of Hezekiah king of Judah," who reigned from 715–686 BC, so the date of the entire collection cannot be from before that time. That means the Instruction of Amenemope could predate the biblical book of Proverbs by as much as five hundred years or more. Nevertheless, as noted by biblical scholar Kenton Sparks, "although Amenemope was composed during the twelfth century BCE, it was copied and studied down into the Late period [i.e., 1100–525 BC], providing ample opportunity for contacts between this text and Israelite wisdom."[5] Because of the earlier date of the Egyptian composition, any borrowing would most likely have been done by Israel.

If this borrowing or influence did occur, it would not necessarily be a unique phenomenon. Agur son of Jakeh, who is cited in Proverbs 30:1 as the author of a number of wisdom sayings and who is mentioned nowhere else in Scripture, may in fact be an Arabian wise man from a tribe related to the Ishmaelites.[6] And what can we say about King Lemuel (31:1), who is also cited as a source of biblical wisdom sayings but is found nowhere else in Scripture? How are we supposed to understand, and can we accept, wisdom writings as Scripture when their origin might be outside of Scripture?

The church has always recognized that God has revealed himself in two different but complementary ways. And because these two ways have the same divine author, they cannot contradict each other. God has revealed truth about himself and his ways in his holy Word (special revelation), and he has also revealed these things to some extent in the structures and processes of creation (general revelation). Perhaps the clearest biblical expression of God's revelation in creation is found in Romans 1:19–20. There the apostle Paul states, "What may be known about God is plain to [people], because God has made it plain to them. For since the creation of the world God's invisible qualities—his eternal power and divine nature—have been clearly seen, being understood from what has been made, so that people are without excuse."

The created world, by divine design, reveals truths about its Creator and the physical and moral order he has infused into his creation. It should not be a surprise, therefore, when others outside the family of God recognize these things as well. In fact, it would be surprising if they didn't. When they get their observations of God's general revelation right, as Amenemope did, their words can be incorporated into God's special revelation as evidence of the universal human ability to recognize the sovereignty of God and the human responsibility to live under his authority.

The fact that these verses of Proverbs may derive from an extrabiblical source has the extraordinary significance of reminding us that God's wisdom is there for all to see, that God floods our senses every day with evidence of his power and divinity. When we share the gospel with others, therefore, we are only elaborating on a testimony that they have been receiving by means of creation over the course of their entire lives.

THINGS TO CONSIDER

1. Many people, Christians and non-Christians, try to persuade us that their way of life is the "wise" way. They may believe they are guided by insights they have gathered from general revelation. Of course, they may have correctly interpreted general revelation or they may have misinterpreted it. How do we determine which? In other words, what objective check is available to distinguish truth from error?

2. What are some examples of contemporary proverbs learned from observing creation and its creatures that align with truths about God and human responsibility to him that we find in Scripture?

3. Do you think it is possible for someone to come to a saving knowledge of God by general revelation alone, or is special revelation necessary as well? Throughout the history of the church, believers have answered this question differently. What does special revelation say about this issue?

19

—o—

Embracing Wisdom

A wife of noble character who can find?
She is worth far more than rubies.
—Proverbs 31:10

On their surface, the final verses of the book of Proverbs appear to be nothing more than a useful guide for young men regarding the kind of wives they should seek and for young women regarding the kind of wives they should aspire to be. But is that all that is going on here? One certainly could not argue against the praiseworthiness of these traits in any woman (or any man, for that matter) or against the wisdom of any young person searching for these attributes in a potential spouse. So using 31:10–31 as a checklist of desired qualities in such a person hardly seems wrong. But doesn't it seem odd that a book whose contents are expressly intended to instruct "the simple" and "the wise" in addition to "the young" (1:4–5) should so drastically narrow down its demographic focus in its last verses to those seeking "a wife of noble character"? Wouldn't we expect this premier biblical book on wisdom to end with some sort of climactic discourse on the necessity and advantage of having wisdom?

As we might have suspected, there are indeed hidden depths of meaning in 31:10–31. And the biblical author has left us clues to this deeper meaning throughout the book of Proverbs, though these may be hidden by an overgrowth of literary subtlety. It's time for us to take out the hedge clippers and cut back some of the obscuring language to see what wonderful things it is hiding from our view.

We begin our hunt for additional depths of meaning in these seemingly ordinary verses about "a wife of noble character" by investigating several other significant places where women are mentioned in the book of Proverbs. And we don't have to read very far at all in the book before we encounter an extended passage where wisdom is depicted as a woman (1:20–33). Like a sidewalk evangelist, she stands in public places and calls out to people who pass by engaged in their meaningless pursuits. She urges them to change course from their self-destructive paths and grasp her extended hand of wisdom so that they can avoid the disaster and calamity that will otherwise overtake them. She invites them instead to follow her advice and "live in safety and be at ease, without fear of harm" (1:33).

The personification of wisdom as a woman is found again several chapters later, in 8:1–36. There she is once more depicted as publicly encouraging everyone to heed her instruction so that they may "find life and receive favor from the LORD" (8:35). This invitation to enjoy the benefits of wisdom extends into the next chapter (9:1–12), where wisdom is again described as a woman who invites the simple to come to her house, eat her food, drink her wine, and enjoy abundant life. This tempting appeal is then contrasted with the invitation from another significant woman in Proverbs—personified folly. She too invites people to her house (9:13–17) to experience what she has to offer. But those unwary souls who yield to her enticements will find themselves headed down a path to ruin (9:18).

In this brief survey of the book of Proverbs, we have discovered that in every place (leaving 31:10–31 aside for the moment) where there is an extended passage featuring a woman as the central figure, the passage is dealing with the *personification* of wisdom or folly *as a woman*. Certainly, then, reading 31:10–31 as also dealing with the personification of wisdom as a woman would be in keeping with the general pattern of the book as a whole. In fact, we might go so far as to say this is the way it *should* be read. But are there any further clues in the book of Proverbs confirming that this is how we should read 31:10–31? And is there any deeper meaning that comes to light when we do? The answer to both of these questions is a resounding yes!

The further clues consist of several textual links the author makes between how he has described wisdom and how he describes the wife of noble character. The first of these textual links is the verb in 31:10. The wife of noble character is someone to "find." The author previously used the same verb to encourage people to "find" personified wisdom (8:17, 35). And even more textual links are found when we consider the words used to describe this wisdom we are urged to find.

Early in the book of Proverbs, the author used feminine terms to describe wisdom—terms that are very similar to those used to describe the wife of noble character:

> Blessed are those who find wisdom,
>> those who gain understanding,
> for *she* is more profitable than silver
>> and yields better returns than gold.
> *She* is more precious than rubies;
>> nothing you desire can compare with *her*.
>> (3:13–15, italics added)

We find the words "more precious than rubies" used again in 8:11:

> Wisdom is *more precious than rubies*,
>> and nothing you desire can compare with her.
>> (italics added)

Surely it is no coincidence that the words used to describe wisdom (portrayed as a desirable woman) in these passages are also found in the passage at the end of the book describing a wife of noble character (31:10). There she is also described as "worth far more than rubies."

One other literary clue strengthens this suspected parallel between wisdom and the wife of noble character. When Lady Wisdom makes her appeal to those passing by (1:20–33), we're told that "at the city gate she makes her speech" (1:21). Similarly, the wife of noble character's works should "bring her praise at the city gate" (31:31). The fact that the activities of these women are both described as taking place at the city gate, where customarily men were in the majority and where legal decisions were made, leads us to suspect that neither passage refers to actual women at all, but rather to the wisdom that should characterize just legal decisions (whether rendered by men or women).

When these pieces of evidence are considered together, the deeper meaning of 31:10–31 becomes clear. The wife of noble character is simply another way to describe Lady Wisdom! The climactic discourse on the necessity and advantage of having wisdom that we expected should end this biblical book on that very subject has been lying there in plain sight all along. Throughout the book of Proverbs, readers are encouraged to seek wisdom, often described in feminine terms. This encouragement culminates in wonderfully rich imagery at the end of the book, where the author urges readers to embrace wisdom as closely as one would embrace a wife! There is no picture of greater intimacy that the author could have chosen than that between a husband and wife. That is the intimacy the author encourages between Lady Wisdom and all who desire to learn from her. And as further encouragement, the author lists all the benefits that wisdom will bring to the person who embraces her. They include the ability to negotiate all the twists and turns of life with the best possible result, enabling a productive life that takes advantage of every opportunity, and a willingness to share hard-earned benefits with those less fortunate. Where wisdom is sorely needed—at the city gate where legal decisions are made—her presence and implementation are praised. There is, indeed, nothing worth seeking more than wisdom.

The New Testament tells us where the wisdom that we should seek can be found in all its fullness. The apostle Paul tells us that in Christ "are hidden all the treasures of wisdom and knowledge" (Col 2:2–3). And for those who believe in him, Christ "has become for us wisdom from God—that is, our righteousness, holiness and redemption" (1 Cor 1:30). Experiencing the benefits of wisdom, then, results from uniting with the one who is the embodiment of wisdom. This is exactly what Proverbs 31:10–31 invites us to do—embrace wisdom as closely as one would embrace a spouse. And the New Testament has shown us that embracing wisdom like that means embracing Christ by faith. When we do, the Holy Spirit begins to transform us into the likeness of Christ so that we will begin to experience the rich and full human experience our Creator made us to enjoy. To become truly wise, then, means embracing and becoming like Jesus. And the consequences of doing so are certainly "worth far more than rubies." A loose paraphrase of 31:10 in light of New Testament revelation would be this:

> Where else could a person find wisdom like the wisdom that comes from a relationship with Jesus Christ? The benefits of that relationship are beyond calculation!

THINGS TO CONSIDER

1. How would you describe a wise person? How does the apostle Paul describe a wise person (1 Cor 1:18–31)? Is your description the same as his? Are there different kinds of wisdom? What kind of wisdom do you strive to attain?

2. Look at all the characteristics of wisdom described in Prov 31:10–31. Consider how all these attributes are true of Christ. Which of these attributes are also true of his church? Which are true of you?

3. Is it possible for a Christian to advance in business, academics, entertainment, or other fields in a society that holds an opposing view of what it means to be wise? Where is the line between adapting to the culture and compromising with it?

20

—○—

THE DEATH OF DEATH

He will swallow up death forever.
—ISAIAH 25:8

N ear the middle of the long prophetic book of Isaiah lies
25:8, whose deeper meaning rests hidden beneath about
two thousand years of dust. The verse already presents us with
a powerful visual image—God swallowing up death—but the
fuller significance of this verse is even more powerful. Perhaps
most contemporary readers don't notice that Isaiah alludes to
what was at that time a well-known cross-cultural figure. When
we take the time to clean off the dust of time so that we can
recognize the allusion Isaiah makes, we'll experience the full
measure of this verse's original potency. However, to get at this
hidden significance, we need to take a field trip beyond the bor-
ders of Israel into the land occupied by one of her ancient Near
Eastern neighbors.

As we've seen in previous chapters,[1] Ugarit is significant for our understanding of Canaanite culture and its potential influence on Israel, due to its geographical and chronological proximity to Israel. The tablets found there provide some insight into the beliefs of the people the Israelites encountered as they took possession of the promised land. One of these insights lifts the veil on the powerful allusion the prophet Isaiah makes in Isaiah 25:8.

Among the many gods the Canaanites worshiped was one who was particularly known for his insatiable appetite. In the mythological literature, we are told that his mouth was unimaginably large, and it seemed that every living thing ultimately and inevitably found its way into it. An epic text discovered at Ugarit provides us with more detail. It concerns a god named Môt, an ancient god of death and the underworld. In one passage of this text is a description of Môt in his own words: "My throat consumes heaps of things, yes indeed, I eat by double handfuls." Later in this same story, the god Baal—a familiar name to readers of the Old Testament—describes Môt even more expansively: "He puts one lip to the earth, the other lip to the heavens, his tongue to the stars."[2] This imagery effectively communicates the fact that nothing escapes Môt's gaping maw, a fact he seems to relish.

This is all very interesting, and perhaps a little frightening, but we need one additional piece of information before we can understand the enormous implications of these cultural details and grasp our verse's deeper meaning. That piece of information comes to us from the humble realm of vocabulary. Hebrew (the language of Isaiah's prophecy) and Ugaritic are related languages. They both belong to the Semitic language family and therefore share many common features, including much of their vocabulary. One of the words they share is the word Môt, which in both Ugaritic (𐎎𐎚) and Hebrew (מות) means "death."

In the Ugaritic texts mentioned previously, we can understand why death has been personified as an all-consuming monster. After all, death may seem to be an all-consuming monster to us today as well. Anyone who has gone through the devastating loss of a loved one or who faces the nightmare of a terminal diagnosis has no trouble at all picturing death as a merciless beast who has a huge mouth that hungrily swallows up life. In fact, we may even feel like all we do is spend our days in an ultimately futile effort to outrun that voracious mouth as long as we can.

Although not going so far as to elevate death to the status of a deity, several biblical texts from the poetic books also personify death (or Môt) as a ravenous monster:

- "Calamity is hungry for him; disaster is ready for him when he falls. It eats away parts of his skin; death's [or Môt's] firstborn devours his limbs." (Job 18:12–13)
- "They are like sheep and are destined to die; death [or Môt] will be their shepherd." (Ps 49:14 [in Hebrew, 49:15])
- "Death [or Môt] and Destruction are never satisfied." (Prov 27:20)

It seems that in Ugarit or Israel or anywhere else, there is no escaping death (or Môt); his mouth is too big and his power is too great. What a welcome prophecy by Isaiah, then, that one day the Sovereign Lord will "swallow up death [or Môt] forever" (Isa 25:8)! The seemingly insatiable swallower whose power seems unopposable will ultimately himself be swallowed up by one who is even more powerful. Even though it may seem, at times, that death will continue its merciless devouring unabated, that is not the case at all. One day its giant mouth will indeed be slammed shut forever.

About seven hundred years after Isaiah wrote this verse, the apostle Paul alluded to it in his first letter to the church at Corinth. Paul agreed with them that it may seem like death is the final reality we all must face. God's law has revealed to us just how far we fall short of being the kind of people who can sustain a relationship with the holy God. And the penalty for our unfaithfulness is death (Rom 6:23). So, apart from some sort of divine intervention, death would indeed have the last word.

But, as Paul goes on to say, God *has* indeed intervened—in the person of Jesus Christ, who paid the terrible price for our sin. This is the heart of the gospel. Consequently, though we may die, death cannot hold us, just as it couldn't hold him (Rom 6:5, 8). We will escape its clutches and rise from the dead to new life—a life that we can begin to experience the benefits of right now. Just as Jesus was victorious over death, so will we be. We have been delivered from sin's penalty (death); and one day we will finally be delivered from its presence as well. Our victory over death is possible only because of Jesus Christ. The apostle Paul put it this way:

> Listen, I tell you a mystery: We will not all sleep, but we will all be changed—in a flash, in the twinkling of an eye, at the last trumpet. For the trumpet will sound, the dead will be raised imperishable, and we will be changed. For the perishable must clothe itself with the imperishable, and the mortal with immortality. When the perishable has been clothed with the imperishable, and the mortal with immortality, then the

saying that is written will come true: "Death has been swallowed up in victory."

> "Where, O death, is your victory?
> Where, O death, is your sting?"

The sting of death is sin, and the power of sin is the law. But thanks be to God! He gives us the victory through our Lord Jesus Christ. (1 Cor 15:51–57)

The prophet Isaiah spoke to God's people during a time of national crisis. Their sin had brought them brokenness, pain, and loss. Isaiah told them that judgment was indeed coming but that they would also experience a restoration in the future. That restoration would involve nothing less than death itself being swallowed up.

What Isaiah dimly saw was the restoration accomplished by the Son of God. Yes, should the Lord delay his return, we will experience death. But death is on borrowed time. Death will ultimately be forced to give way to life because of the drubbing it received on the cross. Jesus proved his victory over this age-old foe by rising from the dead. And his resurrection is a guarantee of our own. And when that happens, "'there will be no more death' or mourning or crying or pain" (Rev 21:4) and our fellowship with God will continue unbroken forever. Until that time, we can borrow the four-hundred-year-old words of John Donne, a poet and cleric in the Church of England, and say to death:

> Death, be not proud, though some have called thee
> Mighty and dreadful, for, thou art not so,

For, those, whom thou think'st, thou dost overthrow
Die not, poor Death, nor yet canst thou kill me. . . .
One short sleep past, we wake eternally,
And death shall be no more, Death thou shalt die.[3]

THINGS TO CONSIDER

1. How does the knowledge that death will ultimately be swallowed up in victory affect the way you face life? What does it mean to be among "those who have been brought from death to life" in Christ (Rom 6:13)?

2. How does the knowledge that death will ultimately be swallowed up in victory affect the way you face death? If Christ defeated death, what does it mean to "die with Christ" (Rom 6:8; Col 2:20)?

3. Does Isaiah's use of a figure from Canaanite mythology to make his point about God disturb you? Is it okay to use references from popular culture when communicating the good news to other people? Are there any dangers in doing so?

21

—o—

THE PATH OF
NO RETURN

"If a man divorces his wife
and she leaves him and marries another man,
should he return to her again?
Would not the land be completely defiled?
But you have lived as a prostitute with
many lovers—
would you now return to me?"
declares the LORD.
—JEREMIAH 3:1

Jeremiah 3:1 poses some tough rhetorical questions to high-light an impossible situation that can be remedied only by a new, unprecedented divine initiative. And the stakes could not be higher. Nothing less than the fate of the whole human race hangs in the balance. Admittedly, to contemporary readers, the gravity of the situation may not be immediately apparent. It may seem that God simply displays here the wounded feelings of a betrayed spouse. It might appear that he is saying something like, "Don't think you can come back to me after you've been unfaithful!" We may think that after appropriate repentance and sacrifice by the guilty party, God would, like so many mistreated human relationship partners, eventually let the bad actor back into the house. But the matter is far more serious, as the hidden aspects of this verse will reveal.

At this time in Israel's history, in the face of their persistent rejection of his guidelines for life, God's long-suffering is wearing thin. As the Lord himself puts it, "They have forsaken my law, which I set before them; they have not obeyed me or followed my law. Instead, they have followed the stubbornness of their hearts; they have followed the Baals, as their ancestors taught them" (Jer 9:13–14). The Lord, through Jeremiah his prophet, urges his people to take this last possible exit on the turnpike before their complete subjugation to foreign powers. Jeremiah is prophesying to them in the dark days immediately before the end of their nation. The Assyrians had already destroyed the Northern Kingdom of Israel, and its people were dispersed throughout the Assyrian Empire. Having outlasted the Assyrians, the Southern Kingdom of Judah now faces Assyria's successors, the Babylonians. They have already repeatedly attacked Judah, forced them to pay massive and humiliating tribute, and exiled large segments of their population to Babylonia. As God's spokesman, Jeremiah has urged, cajoled, and pleaded for his people to return to God in faithful obedience. Now, in 3:1, Jeremiah lays out for the people how desperate their situation truly is.

A hidden depth of meaning in this verse comes to light when we realize Jeremiah is quoting a portion of the book of the law. Not only could this fact be hidden from contemporary Bible readers, but that could even have been the case for the people of Jeremiah's day. That's because the book of the law had lain neglected for decades in the temple and had only recently been rediscovered (2 Kgs 22). The term *book of the law* may refer to the entire Pentateuch (Genesis–Deuteronomy), but at the very least it includes the book of Deuteronomy. And in Deuteronomy 24:1–4, we encounter the very law that Jeremiah is referencing:

> If a man marries a woman who becomes displeasing to him because he finds something indecent about her, and he writes her a certificate of divorce, gives it to her and sends her from his house, and if after she leaves his house she becomes the wife of another man, and her second husband dislikes her and writes her a certificate of divorce, gives it to her and sends her from his house, or if he dies, then her first husband, who divorced her, is not allowed to marry her again after she has been defiled. That would be detestable in the eyes of the LORD. Do not bring sin upon the land the LORD your God is giving you as an inheritance.

Jeremiah references this law because it directly applies to the situation in which God's people would find themselves if they, the last vestige of the covenant community in the promised land, were sent away into exile. Like the wife who is sent away, they would be sent away into exile. And like the wife who unites with another man, they would unite with other gods. According to the law of Deuteronomy, the wife who has been sent away and joined with another man is not allowed to return to her first husband. That would be detestable to the Lord. What logically follows, then, is that if God sends his relationship partner (Judah) into exile and they choose another relationship partner (false gods), God would not be allowed, *by his own law*, to take them back again. In other words, the people of Judah are headed down a path of no return! If they persist in their rebellion against the Lord and are consequently sent away from the land in judgment, then it appears God's relationship with his people would be well and truly over. According to the words of God's own law in Deuteronomy 24:1–4, the answer to the rhetorical questions of Jeremiah 3:1 ("Should he [God] return to [Judah]?" and "Would you . . . return to me?") is "Certainly not!" God *could not* take Judah back, and Judah *could not* return to God, even if they wanted to.

This is therefore a critically momentous time for Judah. But it is also a critically important time for every other human being because salvation was to come to the world through the Jews (John 4:22). If God's relationship with them comes to an end, what hope would any human being have? God had promised that all peoples on earth would be blessed through the line of Abraham (Gen 12:1–3). Moreover, the Messiah was prophesied to come through the line of Abraham's descendant Judah (Gen 49:10–12; Isa 11:1–10). If all that is left of the nation of Judah is sent away into exile—and that certainly appears probable at this point in their history—what hope do they have and what hope do any of us have for any possible relationship with God in the future? That hope seems all but extinguished according to God's own law. After all, he cannot contradict himself.

Another hidden aspect of this verse that follows from the apparent insuperability of God's law is the implication that if there were to be any hope at all, it would have to originate with God. Not that there is any reason to expect such a superfluity of grace. But, incomprehensibly, that's exactly what happens.

In the midst of this seemingly hopeless situation, Jeremiah prophesies something extraordinary—a way out of this legal and relational conundrum. He prophesies that God will unilaterally initiate a *new* covenant, or relationship, with his people. And this new relationship will not be like the old one, which "they broke . . . , though I [God] was a husband to them" (Jer 31:32). So this promised new relationship will be different from the old one in that it will no longer be capable of being broken! This sounds fantastic, but perhaps too good to be true. After all, how can such a relationship possibly exist? Won't any relationship that God enters into with human beings ultimately be doomed to failure from the start because of the inability of humans, any humans, to live up to their part of the relationship?

The only way to have an unbreakable relationship is if there is a perfectly faithful relationship partner on both sides of the equation. And the only perfectly faithful relationship partner is God himself. Therefore, for an unbreakable relationship to exist, God himself would have to fulfill the responsibilities of both sides of it. This is the essence of the new covenant that God promises through Jeremiah. God would become a human being through the incarnation of Jesus Christ in order to do what no other human being could—perfectly obey the will of the Father. Now for all those who unite with Jesus by faith, he is their representative in this new God-human relationship, a relationship that is no longer doomed to fail. Instead of a relationship between God and man, the new covenant is a relationship between God and the God-man, Jesus Christ, and all those who unite with that

God-man by faith. For those who do, their relationship with the Father is just as secure as the Father's relationship with the Son.

God, with ingenious and amazing grace, devised a workaround for the intractable problem of our human rebelliousness. The rhetorical questions of Jeremiah 3:1 lead us into the deeper waters of God's revealed and steadfast love that comes to expression in the new covenant relationship made possible by Jesus's perfect obedience to the will of the Father on our behalf, including his full payment of the awful penalty for our disobedience.

Only when we realize that we, like Judah, are incapable of faithfully and consistently living as God has directed will we turn to the gracious provision he has made for us through his own Son. God's relentless love has made a way for a relationship with him despite our relentless rebellion. Exploring the hidden depths of meaning of Jeremiah 3:1 has revealed the very heart of the gospel. Why God would choose to love us this way and this much, however, remains hidden.

THINGS TO CONSIDER

1. When Jeremiah prophesied, the Babylonians were the mightiest nation on earth. In human terms, the nation of Judah did not have even a tenth of their power. If you had lived then, who do you think would have had more influence on you? The Babylonians, who had repeatedly attacked and defeated you? Or some religious figure who was at odds with the statements of most religious leaders and espoused views contrary to official government positions?

2. Today, scientific humanism and materialism are the dominant views in society. In human terms, the church does not have a tenth of their influence. Who has more influence on you? Those scientists, educators, and social icons who control every aspect of the culture? Or religious figures who call people back to seemingly antiquarian belief in and obedience to the God of the Bible?

3. Jeremiah's prophecy reminds us that God alone could and did ensure that the conditions of his covenant were finally and fully met by sending his Son to fulfill those conditions for us in a new relationship, a new covenant, that can never be broken. Does this amazing demonstration of God's love for you encourage your own faithful obedience? Or does the fact that Jesus fulfills the covenant on our behalf discourage your own faithful obedience?

22

—o—

Break Time

*"Then break the jar while those who
go with you are watching."*
—Jeremiah 19:10

To readers today, what God directs the prophet Jeremiah to do in Jeremiah 19:10 might seem excessive (although consistent with Jeremiah's personality), but Jeremiah's actions add force and memorability to his message of judgment. His behavior is perhaps comparable to a contemporary Sunday morning worship service in which a dramatic presentation helps to communicate the point of the pastor's message. And we would not be wrong to regard Jeremiah's actions in this way. But there is another depth of significance to Jeremiah's behavior that takes the implications of his jar-smashing activity to a whole other level.

At the beginning of the chapter, God commands Jeremiah to "go and buy a clay jar from a potter" (19:1). Then God directs

Jeremiah to take along the leaders of the people and go to the Valley of Ben Hinnom, where he is to deliver a scathing indictment of their sins, chief of which are their unfaithfulness and rebellion against the Lord. Jeremiah then must follow his prosecution of God's case against his people with a pronouncement of the judgment to come. At this climactic point in Jeremiah's oration, God directs him to smash the jar and explain to his people the significance of doing so: "This is what the LORD Almighty says: I will smash this nation and this city just as this potter's jar is smashed and cannot be repaired" (19:11). All of this seems straightforward enough, even if it is more than a little unsettling. The smashed jar is a visual complement to Jeremiah's verbal message of judgment. But the people of Jeremiah's day would have registered a more profound and ominous depth of significance to his actions. This deeper meaning derives from a practice observed in Egypt, their neighbor to the south.

Israel had spent over four hundred years in Egypt (Exod 12:40)—more than ten generations. Over such a long time, they no doubt observed, were very familiar with, and perhaps even adopted many of the practices of their host country. One of the Egyptian practices they would have encountered involved ceremonies in which official ritual cursings (called execrations) would take place. World-renowned Egyptologist Robert K. Ritner explains further:

> From the Old Kingdom through the Roman era, priests performed official ritual cursings of the potential enemies of Egypt. The ceremonies included the breaking of red pots and figurines inscribed with formal "Execration Texts" listing

Nubians, Asiatics, Libyans, living and deceased Egyptians, as well as generally threatening forces. The texts themselves contain no explicit curses, but instead serve to identify the fate of the enemies with that of the destroyed pot or image.[1]

By smashing the clay jar while the leaders of Israel looked on, Jeremiah brought this Egyptian practice to their minds once again, and there could be no doubt about its implications. As biblical scholar and translator Steven Voth notes,

> The imagery here is one of destruction for the Israelites and their capital city, Jerusalem. This kind of image was common in the ancient Near East. . . . The Egyptians practiced magical cursing against their present or potential enemies by inscribing pottery bowls with the name of their enemies and then smashing them. This served as a poignant symbolic action, similar to Jeremiah's actions here.[2]

Because this ritual practice involved smashing pottery, examples of the things being cursed on that pottery are difficult to come by today. Nevertheless, such examples do exist and give us a picture of the "present or potential enemies" whose power was believed to be magically broken along with the pottery. Among the cursed were all those within the land who participated in or fomented rebellion, as one execration text specifies: "All men, all people, all folk, all males, all eunuchs, all women, and all officials, who may rebel, who may plot, who may fight, who may talk of fighting, or who may talk of rebelling—in this entire land."[3] Not only were such rebellious people ritually cursed in this way, but another execration text even lists the internal motivations and external evidences of their rebellion that were cursed as well: "Every evil word, every evil speech, every evil slander, every evil thought, every evil plot, every evil fight, every evil quarrel, every evil plan, every evil thing, all evil dreams, and all evil slumber."[4]

Smashing pottery was such an appropriate and effective object lesson for Jeremiah's rebellious audience to see! The Lord had repeatedly charged them with rebellion (Jer 2:8, 29; 3:13; 4:17; 6:28; 14:7). In fact, the agents of rebellion and the evidence of their rebellion described in the Egyptian execration texts are summarized in 6:28 and applied to God's people:

> They are all hardened rebels,
> going about to slander.
> They are bronze and iron;
> they all act corruptly.

This was the situation in Jeremiah's day. God's people had become as receptive to God's word as bronze and iron. The curse of judgment had become inevitable.

The location where Jeremiah was sent to perform his symbolic jar smashing—the Valley of Ben Hinnom—suggests further that the coming judgment would be appropriate to the sin God's people had committed. This valley was associated with cultic service to foreign gods, especially the heinous practice of sacrificing children in the fire to the pagan gods Baal and Molek.[5] Such gruesome burning is the source of the New Testament references[6] to Gehenna (γεεννα [geenna], often translated as "hell"), based on the Greek equivalent of the Hebrew גֵּיא הִנֹּם (gê' hinnōm), the Valley of Hinnom. Those who participated in this grotesque practice, or the rebellious nature that spawned it, would themselves ultimately be judged by fire (Rev 20:14–15).

The deeper significance of Jeremiah 19:10, therefore, is the seriousness of the situation God's people find themselves in, communicated to them not only verbally but also visually by means of the foreign ritual practice of smashing pottery to indicate the fate of the wrongdoers. Like the names on the Egyptian pottery that could anticipate the same fate as the smashed pot, so Jeremiah's audience could envision their own names divinely written on the pottery Jeremiah was smashing and realize that they too were cursed.

By God's grace, the story does not end with this verse. Through Jeremiah, God promises a new covenant, or relationship, in which he "will forgive their wickedness and will remember their sins no more" (31:34). But we may wonder how such a radical shift could be possible. How could God's people change from the object of his cursing to the object of his forgiveness? Certainly, the judgment would come against Jeremiah's people in the form of exile, but that would hardly exhaust God's wrath against their sin or justify this gracious turn to divine mercy. The answer to this dilemma, the New Testament informs us, is the arrival of a representative substitute for the objects of the divine curse.

The apostle Paul tells us that Jesus came to be, in our place, the shattered object of the divine curse: "Christ redeemed us from the curse of the law by becoming a curse for us, for it is written: 'Cursed is everyone who is hung on a pole'" (Gal 3:13). Jesus serves, in effect, as the clay jar in the execration ritual. That is, just as the names of all the rebels and their rebellious acts were written on the clay jar that was shattered in the place of judgment, so the names of all the rebels and their rebellious acts were ascribed to Jesus, who was "crushed for our iniquities" (Isa 53:5) in the place of judgment.

And for all those who by faith claim him as their representative, just as their rebellion is ascribed to him, so his righteousness is ascribed to them. As the apostle Paul put it, "God made him who had no sin to be sin for us, so that in him we might become the righteousness of God" (2 Cor 5:21). Unlike the pagan execration ritual, which hopes for a magical resolution to perceived woes, Jesus not only bears the curse of divine judgment himself but also replaces it within each believer with the Spirit of righteousness. This is the Spirit that effectuates the new relationship, or covenant, with God that Jeremiah prophesied (Jer 31:33) as lying on the other side of divine judgment. In the words of Paul: "The Spirit you received does not make you slaves, so that you live in fear again; rather, the Spirit you received brought about your adoption to sonship. And by him we cry, 'Abba, Father'" (Rom 8:15). By being broken for us, Jesus makes us whole.

THINGS TO CONSIDER

1. Does it trouble you that God directed Jeremiah to use a magical ritual from a foreign nation to get his message across to the Israelites? How might God's use of such an execration ritual be a further indictment of his people's polytheism? How does the place Jeremiah is commanded to perform this ritual corroborate this?

2. If you lived in ancient Egypt and were going to engage in an execration ritual of your own, whose names and what offensive acts would you write down on your clay jar? Might anyone write *your* name or actions on their own clay jar?

3. The names and behaviors of rebels were written on the clay jars to be smashed in the belief that what happened to the jars would happen to the rebels. What does it mean for your name to be written on Christ? What does it mean for his name to be written on you?

23

—o—

THE DESIGNATED
DRINKER

*"Take from my hand this cup filled with
the wine of my wrath and make all the
nations to whom I send you drink it."*
—JEREMIAH 25:15

Many of us are familiar with the term *designated driver.* It refers to the individual whom partygoers single out as the one who will not partake in alcoholic beverages during the evening's festivities so as to be able to safely drive others home afterward. What we encounter in Jeremiah 25:15 is exactly the opposite. God is instructing Jeremiah to make designated nations drink. But what these specified nations are required to drink is alarming—if you're one of them. And that's where the surprising significance of this verse begins to manifest itself.

Crucial to our accessing the deeper meaning of this verse is understanding how the Bible uses the imagery of the cup. The image of a cup sometimes has positive connotations. Consider, for example, its use in Psalm 23:5: "You anoint my head with oil; my cup overflows."[1] However, the use of a cup in the Bible to signify something desirable is quite rare. By far the most common connotation of the biblical cup imagery, and without question the connotation found in Jeremiah 25:15, is that of judgment. The Old Testament often uses imagery of a cup filled with the wine of God's wrath that the wicked are forced to drink. Consider, for example, the following verses:

> Let their own eyes see their destruction;
> > let them [i.e., the wicked] drink the cup of the
> > > wrath of the Almighty. (Job 21:20)

> In the hand of the Lord is a cup
> > full of foaming wine mixed with spices;
> he pours it out, and all the wicked of the earth
> > drink it down to its very dregs. (Ps 75:8)

> The cup from the Lord's right hand is coming
> > around to you [Babylon],
> and disgrace will cover your glory. (Hab 2:16)[2]

So when the Israelites heard Jeremiah mention the cup filled with the wine of God's wrath, they might very well have felt a sense of relief, believing that those who would have to experience such a judgment must certainly be enemies of God and his people. After all, the verses just prior to Jeremiah 25:15 referred to God's judgment against Babylon, the nation that was causing Israel so much grief. Finally, the Israelites might have thought, our enemies will get what they deserve! And it is true that Israel's enemies are included in the list of people groups who would "drink, get drunk and vomit, and fall to rise no more because of the sword [God] will send among [them]" (25:27). But what would have been alarmingly unexpected for the Israelites to learn is that they too were included among those who would have to drink from the cup of God's wrath. In fact, they headed the list! Among the designated drinkers of the cup filled with the wine of God's wrath are "Jerusalem and the towns of Judah, its kings and officials, to make them a ruin and an object of horror and scorn, a curse—as they are today" (25:18).

As unsettling as it is to read about God including his own people on the list of those who would experience his judgment, most of us today might not be too concerned just yet. After all, we may rationalize, we aren't Israelites or enemies of the Israelites. So what do Jeremiah's words have to do with us? But before we too quickly dismiss Jeremiah's words as irrelevant to us, we should note that his prophecy concerning this cup of God's wrath is full of catchall phrases that make it abundantly clear that it applies not just to some people at some time in ancient history but to every human being. There is no one who has not sinned and who is not a designated drinker of the cup filled with God's punishment for that sin. Jeremiah says God's judgment will extend to "all the kingdoms on the face of the earth" (25:26) and that God "is calling down a sword on all who live on the earth" (25:29). In other words, this cup filled with the wine of God's wrath represents fearsome divine judgment on the sin of every human being on the face of the earth—past, present, and future. Now things just got real. If every human being deserves to drink from the cup of God's wrath, then what hope is there for anyone?

That question would remain hanging in the air like the sword of Damocles for about six hundred years until it was answered by Jesus himself in his prayer to the Father on the Mount of Olives just before he was arrested and crucified. His disciples had accompanied him there, but he left them by themselves for some time so that he could pray in solitude regarding the excruciating ordeal that he would uniquely face. His prayer was anguished, arduous, and earnest, evidenced by the "sweat . . . like drops of blood" that attended it and by the angelic support necessary to strengthen him in it (Luke 22:43–44). It is in this context of torment that Jesus uttered the words of verse 42: "Father, if you are willing, take this cup from me; yet not my will, but yours be done." Now that we have some understanding of the biblical imagery of the cup, the deeper significance of what Jesus prays comes into sharper focus. And that significance has everything to do with what Jeremiah had prophesied so many years before.

Jesus referred to the same cup as that in Jeremiah's prophecy, the cup filled with the wine of God's wrath. We can only imagine the horror of God's wrath against every human sin ever committed. But Jesus didn't have to imagine. He knew exactly what was coming as he prayed alone in the dark on that awful evening. He realized fully what it would mean to drink down the unrestrained torrent of divine wrath against the sin of every person who had ever lived or would ever live. It is no wonder Jesus prayed that, if possible, the Father would take such a cup away from him!

This cup imagery reappears at other crucial times in Jesus's final hours. Indeed, only minutes after his prayer to the Father,

Jesus's resolve to bear this unimaginable punishment is evidenced by his response to Peter's armed resistance to the detachment who had come to arrest Jesus: "Put your sword away! Shall I not drink the cup the Father has given me?" (John 18:11). And this fuller understanding of the cup imagery also unlocks a greater depth of meaning to Jesus's words uttered earlier that evening. At the Last Supper, Jesus said to his disciples, "This cup is the new covenant in my blood, which is poured out for you" (Luke 22:20). Jesus was no doubt referring to the physical cup that he was holding in his hand, but at the same time he was also referring to the cup filled with the wine of God's wrath. Only by taking that punishment on himself (which he refers to as "my blood") could the new, unbreakable relationship with God (which he calls "the new covenant") be made possible.

Jesus's willingness to experience on behalf of human beings the terrible consequences of the sin for which we alone are responsible is at the heart of the gospel. It is an amazing expression of gracious self-sacrifice and love so great as to exceed our ability to comprehend it. As the apostle Paul put it, "Very rarely will anyone die for a righteous person, though for a godly person someone might possibly dare to die. But God demonstrates his own love for us in this: While we were still sinners, Christ died for us" (Rom 5:7–8). That Jesus was, in fact, willing to stand in our place under God's judgment merits our continual thanksgiving and praise to him.

This reflection on the imagery of the cup leads each one of us to a binary decision that has eternal consequences. The divine penalty for human sin must and will be paid. As Jeremiah put it, God is "calling down a sword on all who live on the earth" (Jer 25:29). There is no evading, postponing, or nullifying this penalty. And so the cup of God's wrath comes around to each one of us. We must decide how that payment for our sin will take place. On behalf of all who will receive it by faith, Jesus drank to the dregs the wine of the cup of God's wrath against the sin of every human being. So the choice before us is clear. We either unite with Jesus by faith, claiming him as our representative, so that his payment for sin counts as ours (i.e., we let him be the designated drinker of the cup of God's wrath for us), or we refuse what Jesus has done for us and consequently opt to pay the price for our sin (i.e., drink the cup of God's wrath) ourselves. Those are the only two options. May God give us the understanding and courage to choose wisely so that we no longer have to drink from that terrifying cup.

THINGS TO CONSIDER

1. At the Lord's Supper, when we "eat this bread and drink this cup, [we] proclaim the Lord's death until he comes" (1 Cor 11:26). Consider how our drinking from the cup is a way of proclaiming to the Lord that we embrace his drinking the cup for us. How could you encourage other believers with this truth?

2. Reflect on what Jesus faced that night as he prayed on the Mount of Olives. It is hard enough to imagine the horrors of eternal judgment against our own sin, much less the judgment against the sin of every human being. But our understanding is impeded by our human limitations. Consider how much more clearly the Son of God

understood the full implications of what was in store for him. Does his willingness to go through it anyway inform and strengthen your gratitude?

3. The cup filled with the wine of God's wrath must be drunk by "all who live on the earth" (Jer 25:29). There are only two options available for each human being to accomplish this horrifying task: allow Jesus to be our designated drinker or drink it ourselves. Does knowing this affect the urgency with which you communicate the gospel to your family and friends? Is it possible for you to comprehend the magnitude of what Jesus has done for you and not share this with other people?

24

—○—

THE BIGGER THEY ARE

And after all of them, the king of
Sheshak will drink it too.
—JEREMIAH 25:26

I n almost exactly the middle of the longest book of the Bible (by word count in the original language), we encounter Jeremiah 25:26, which contains a highly significant detail we might read over without even noticing. It is, effectively, hidden in plain sight. One reason we might miss this detail is because the verse is situated in a frightful context of divine wrath. It comes at a point in Jeremiah's prophecy where he announces the terrible judgment that God will unleash against sin. As we saw in the last chapter, Jeremiah evocatively describes that judgment as a cup filled with the wine of God's wrath that all the guilty parties will be forced to take and drink. And drinking from this goblet of doom will cause those who imbibe to "fall to rise no more" (25:27).

In 25:18–26, Jeremiah enumerates those who have been found guilty in God's court of law. After the startling and unsettling discovery of God's own people at the head of that list ("Jerusalem and the towns of Judah"), we continue reading a long list of eighteen other specific people groups, as well as general descriptions of people located in "coastlands across the sea" (v. 22), "distant places" (v. 23), "the wilderness" (v. 24), and "the north" (v. 26). The list leaves no doubt that the ones who deserve the terrible divine judgment for their sin are all human beings on the planet. It is therefore surprising and seemingly redundant to see yet another name appended to the end of the list *after* "all the kingdoms on the face of the earth" (v. 26). After all, who could possibly be left? Here is where our mystery begins and where we begin our work of uncovering the deeper meaning of our verse.

The prophet Jeremiah says that after all the kingdoms on the face of the earth have received their just punishment, described as drinking from the cup filled with the wine of God's wrath, "the king of Sheshak will drink it too" (v. 26). There are two issues we must resolve in order to understand the deeper meaning of this verse: (1) Where is Sheshak? and (2) Why does this place get singled out for special consideration?

Let's begin with the first question. Everywhere else in Jeremiah's list where "the king of *X*" is listed, *X* refers to some known geographical location. For example, when the king of Egypt, the kings of Tyre and Sidon, and the kings of Arabia are mentioned, we have no trouble locating Egypt, Tyre and Sidon, and Arabia on a map. So when Jeremiah refers to the king of Sheshak, we expect to be able to locate Sheshak on a map as well. But a quick check of any Bible atlas reveals that no geographical place with the name Sheshak existed anywhere in the ancient

Near East! That's the first clue that this name signifies something else, something deeper. Further complicating the issue is that in the entire Bible this name occurs only in the prophecy of Jeremiah (here and 51:41). The key to solving the puzzle is an ingenious Hebrew cryptographic writing called 'atbash.

In Hebrew, 'atbash writing encodes the language by replacing the first consonant of the alphabet (א, transliterated into English as ') with the last consonant (ת, transliterated into English as t), the second consonant of the alphabet (ב, transliterated into English as b) with the second-to-last consonant (שׁ, transliterated into English as sh), and so forth. The very term 'atbash is a manufactured name that provides the key to how the substitution scheme works: the first two letters of the Hebrew alphabet (א and ב, ' and b) are each immediately followed by the consonant that replaces them. The ת (or t) replaces the א (or ') and so follows immediately after it, and the שׁ (or sh) replaces the ב (or b) and so follows immediately after it. An a vowel is inserted between the consonant pairs to make the word pronounceable and voilà: 'atbash.

Now we can apply our knowledge of 'atbash writing to reverse engineer what is being encoded by the word Sheshak. The sh is the second-to-last consonant in the Hebrew alphabet, so we'll replace that consonant with the second consonant of the alphabet: b. And because sh occurs two times in Sheshak, we'll replace the sh with b one more time. The k with which the name ends is the eleventh consonant in the Hebrew alphabet, so we'll replace that consonant with the eleventh-from-the-last consonant of the alphabet: l. The decoded consonants of sh–sh–k, then, become b–b–l. These are the consonants for the Hebrew word for Babylon (בָּבֶל bābel)! In Hebrew, Babylon is written with an a vowel followed by an *e* vowel. As in *'atbash* writing of consonants, these are reversed as well, resulting in an *e* vowel followed by an *a* vowel, which is what we have in the name Sheshak. Jeremiah is saying, therefore, that after all the people of every nation on the face of the earth have experienced God's judgment, the king of Babylon will experience it too.

But this leaves us with the question of why Jeremiah would use *'atbash* writing to encode the name of Babylon. After all, Babylon is found many times elsewhere in his prophecy (e.g., 20:4, 5, 6; 21:2, 4, 7, 10). The possible answer to this question has two parts. First, we can well understand why Jeremiah would encode the name of the powerful enemy who would destroy his nation and perhaps be able to subsequently read the prophecies Jeremiah had leveled against him. Why wouldn't Jeremiah communicate his prophecy against Babylon in a way that was perfectly clear to his fellow citizens but wouldn't bring unnecessary grief to himself? Second, while it is true that there are many explicit references to Babylon in Jeremiah's prophecy, most of them are in contexts that do not involve divine judgment against its king. Instead, they simply describe what the king of Babylon is doing or even encourage the people of Judah to surrender to him and serve him. Only in chapter 50 is there an extended passage that mentions God's coming judgment of Babylon, where the place name is explicitly and repeatedly mentioned. So if Jeremiah is willing to specifically name Babylon in chapter 50, why does he use coded language to do so in 25:26? Some suggest that "Jeremiah might have resorted to the code name while Nebuchadnezzar was at the gates of Jerusalem."[1] Perhaps as the threat from Babylon grew more imminent, Jeremiah began to encode the name of this foe in his condemnation of them.

We have one more question to consider before we can completely remove the veil that has concealed the full depth of meaning of this verse: Why is Babylon singled out like this in Jeremiah's prophecy of divine judgment? Jeremiah has already given an all-inclusive statement about who deserves to drink this cup of God's wrath. Why go back and highlight this one nation? At least part of the answer is that this is the nation that would bring to an end the last remaining presence of God's people in the promised land. It would be tempting for the king of Babylon to suppose that he was mightier than the God the Israelites served, that God was not able to protect his people in the face of Babylon's overwhelming power. It might even be tempting for the Israelites to think similar thoughts as they went into exile, trudging along more than eight hundred miles from Jerusalem to Babylon! To dispel any such notions, the king of Babylon needed to be made aware (as did God's own people) that his own time for divine judgment was coming as well. But there is even more to consider regarding Jeremiah's special mention of Babylon.

In New Testament imagery, Babylon is "understood as the archetypal head of all entrenched worldly resistance to God."[2] The apostle John uses the term *Babylon* in this figurative way in the book of Revelation. And he alludes to this very passage in Jeremiah's prophecy when he does so: "The great city split into three parts, and the cities of the nations collapsed. God remembered Babylon the Great and gave her the cup filled with the wine of the fury of his wrath" (Rev 16:19).

It is against this archetype of all earthly rebellion against God that Jesus did battle and overcame on the cross, ensuring the ultimate downfall of every kingdom except his own. The choice between the kingdom of Babylon and the kingdom of God is one every person must make. Will we by faith join Jesus's kingdom, trusting that the terrible divine judgment he experienced on the cross applies to us, or will we join the kingdom of Babylon, rejecting Jesus's payment for our sins and sharing in the ultimate downfall of "Babylon the Great," who, John tells us, "will be consumed by fire, for mighty is the Lord God who judges her" (Rev 18:8)? When times are hard, as they were for God's people when facing Babylonian exile, it is tempting to surrender to the thinking of those who seem to be in control. But Jeremiah reminds us, as does John in the New Testament, that those who rebel against God and oppress his people cannot escape the cup of divine judgment that is coming to them. For even someone as seemingly invincible as the king of Sheshak will drink it too.

THINGS TO CONSIDER

1. How does it make you feel to know that everyone who opposes God and his people will ultimately experience God's judgment? Do you feel relief? Joy? Sorrow? How does it make you feel to know that we all deserve God's judgment?

2. In Jeremiah's day, by all human standards, Babylon appeared to be the mightiest force on earth and so was a fitting representative of all seemingly insuperable threats to God's people and challenges to God's authority. What do you think best represents those threats today?

3. Imagine you lived among God's people in Jeremiah's day. Do you think you would have been able to continue to believe that God was in control? In your circumstances today, who seems to be in control, Babylon (figuratively speaking) or God? What could encourage you to continue to trust in God, even during the difficult and confusing times?

25

—o—

CRUMBLING
INTO CHAOS

Without pity the Lord has swallowed up
all the dwellings of Jacob;
in his wrath he has torn down
the strongholds of Daughter Judah.
He has brought her kingdom and its princes
down to the ground in dishonor.
—LAMENTATIONS 2:2

Perhaps you've been there, standing in front of the card rack looking in vain for the perfect card to send to a friend whose world has been destroyed by tragedy. In your search you realize just how inadequate are the few lines the greeting card company provides. And so it is with Lamentations 2:2, which only begins to capture the magnitude of the upheaval to the author's world that he is responding to in this biblical book. The extent of the cataclysm is so wide reaching and so foundation shaking that it simply cannot be communicated by the words of a single verse. So, in a departure from the literary techniques we've considered in previous chapters, here the biblical author has matched the extent of the calamity with the extent of his description, which fills *the entire book*. In both form and content, the book of Lamentations powerfully communicates the comprehensiveness of the disaster that befell the nation. This is the hidden depth of meaning of this part of divine revelation that we will investigate further in this chapter.

Indeed, most of us can't even begin to imagine the trauma experienced by God's people when the Babylonians overran their land in 586 BC and brought their lives as they knew them to a miserable end. God's chosen nation, Judah, and its capital city, Jerusalem—the place God had designated for his holy temple—had been reduced to an inconsequential footnote in the annals of the world's great empires. As the author of Lamentations put it in the book's first verse,

> How deserted lies the city,
>> once so full of people!
> How like a widow is she,
>> who once was great among the nations!
> She who was queen among the provinces
>> has now become a slave. (1:1)

For those who escaped death, every detail of their lives had changed. Like concentric circles collapsing from the outside in, everything they had mistakenly looked to for security and stability fell away, leaving them feeling abandoned, vulnerable, and helpless.

Their outermost circle of security, the allies they believed they could rely on in times of trouble, proved worse than worthless when tested (1:2, 17, 19). Moving inward, we encounter the next circle of security, a literal one—the city's walls. But not even these could stand against the Babylonian onslaught (2:8, 9). One might hope that the next layer of security, the sturdiest buildings of the city—the palaces and strongholds—might endure. But these too fell in the face of the Lord's wrath (2:5). If one looked for help from the officials, whose chief task was to ensure the safety of their people, one would have been sorely disappointed, for they had "fled before the pursuer" (1:6), been exiled (2:9), or been executed (5:12). One might hope that even without government buildings or leaders the nation could still survive. After all, they had done so for many years during the time of the judges. As long as God protected them and they could take comfort in the security of their religious traditions, their lives could retain some sort of recognizable order. But it was not to be. The Babylonians ransacked the temple (1:10), demonstrating that the Lord had "rejected his altar and abandoned his sanctuary" (2:7). Both priests and prophets were killed (2:20). Finally, even the seemingly inviolable sources of personal security, one's home and family, could not withstand the catastrophe. The Babylonians confiscated homes (5:2) and tore apart families, leaving orphans, widows (5:3), violated women (5:11), and enslaved young men (5:13).

The author of Lamentations has endeavored to use words to describe a disaster for which there really are no words. How can anyone adequately respond to an event that has removed all sense of what is familiar or safe? As anyone knows who has had their world turned upside down and their life shattered by devastating loss, illness, or betrayal, the old realities don't seem to apply anymore. Every day just seems to be a continual struggle toward a pointless future. How can someone effectively convey the despair they feel when their world has crumbled into chaos? Our author has done so by beginning with a literary form that itself crumbles into chaos as the book progresses. Before we see how he has done this, we need to learn more about this literary form he has used so skillfully—the acrostic.

Every chapter of Lamentations uses an alphabetic acrostic, a literary device found in the Hebrew Bible that might not be apparent to readers limited by the translation of Hebrew into English. In this literary form, the twenty-two letters of the Hebrew alphabet are used as the format for poetic expression. So in chapter 1, the first verse begins with the first letter of the Hebrew alphabet (א *aleph*); the second verse begins with the second letter (ב *bet*); and so forth until the last, twenty-second, verse of the chapter, which begins with the last letter (ת *tav*). Everything is orderly, just like the author's world seemed to be before the Babylonians arrived. But cracks in the established and reassuring order begin to appear already in chapter 2.

In chapter 2 we again encounter an acrostic of twenty-two verses in which each verse begins with the corresponding letter of the Hebrew alphabet . . . almost. There is a problem with letters sixteen and seventeen (ע [*ayin*] and פ [*pe*]). These two letters have been reversed. By introducing a small measure of disorder into an extremely orderly composition, the author has used the *form* of his lament to underscore its *content*. Just as disorder has begun to appear in the alphabetic sequence, so also disorder has begun to appear in the author's world. Now, someone might suspect that this deviation was accidental, a minor slip that hardly warrants serious consideration. That argument would have more weight, however, if exactly the same thing weren't also present in the next two acrostics, chapters 3 and 4.

Chapter 3 forms the center of the five chapters of the book. Its pivotal position is highlighted by the fact that each letter of the Hebrew alphabet receives three verses, for a total of sixty-six. In this acrostic, just as in chapter 2, the verses beginning with *ayin* and *pe* have been reversed. This is also the case in chapter 4, which reverts back to a single verse for each Hebrew letter.

Finally, we arrive at chapter 5, which also has the same number of verses as letters in the Hebrew alphabet. Though the number of the verses suggests some relationship to an alphabetic acrostic, there is no discernible alphabetic order. Many letters are repeated, and eleven do not appear at all at the beginning of the verses. In both form and content, the author has brought readers to the place where he himself has come, a place so charged with chaos that seemingly even the structure of the alphabet has not survived! The depths of his heartrending melancholy are felt in the final verse of the book, where after an appeal for restoration, the author audaciously but honestly questions the compassion of God: ". . . unless you have utterly rejected us and are angry with us beyond measure" (5:22).

But the author has provided an answer to his own heartfelt question regarding God's compassion, and he has done this within his ingenious acrostics. We saw that the middle acrostic, chapter 3, differs from the rest in that three verses are given to each Hebrew letter. The middle letter (כ *kaph*) of this middle acrostic forms the center of the entire book and in this pivotal position sets a floor for the depths of depression expressed by the surrounding laments. The central truth of these three verses, around which the entire book turns, is that whatever else may change, however many layers of our false security get stripped away, one fundamental truth remains rock steady, unchanging forever:

> No one is cast off
>> by the Lord forever.
> Though he brings grief, he will show compassion,
>> so great is his unfailing love.
> For he does not willingly bring affliction
>> or grief to anyone. (3:31–33)

God's perpetually unfailing love means that whatever punishment he brings against his people because of their sin is always tempered by his mercy.

Later in redemptive history, that same unfailing love of God would become incarnate in Jesus Christ. In God's mercy, Jesus experienced on our behalf the divine punishment that we had merited and he had not. For all those who trust in him, God's judgment against their sin is now satisfied. There is no more price to be paid. And there is nothing that can separate us from God's love—no foreign invaders, no national collapse, no government shutdown, no loss of employment, no financial ruin, no pandemic. The apostle Paul expanded on the central verse of Lamentations in his letter to the church at Rome, a believing community subject to Roman imperial rule and that would soon experience the horrors of religious persecution: "I am convinced that neither death nor life, neither angels nor demons, neither the present nor the future, nor any powers, neither height nor depth, nor anything else in all creation, will be able to separate us from the love of God that is in Christ Jesus our Lord" (Rom 8:38–39).

The hidden Hebrew literary device used so extensively by the author of Lamentations adds a depth to our understanding of this biblical book. The disintegrating acrostic that highlights the magnitude of the devastation that the people of God can and did experience also highlights the magnitude of the compassion of God that steadfastly remains even in the midst of it. Circumstances may quickly change from what we consider normal to a chaos that we could never have imagined, but the compassion of God will never change. The New Testament encourages believers to shift their focus from those changing circumstances to the unchanging God of all compassion (e.g., 2 Cor 1:3).

THINGS TO CONSIDER

1. The author of Lamentations mourned the consequences of God's judgment against the nation's faithlessness. Now that Jesus has paid the price for our faithlessness, do you think it is right that Christians should face hardships? Jesus was perfectly faithful. Do you think it was right that *he* faced hardships? How can God's "compassions never fail" (Lam 3:22) while his people suffer?

2. Jesus said, "I have told you these things, so that in me you may have peace. In this world you will have trouble"

(John 16:33). What do you think Jesus meant by that? Do you think it is possible to have peace and trouble at the same time? If so, how? Is it true in your own life?

3. How should a believer pray about their own or others' hardship? In other words, should the lament of a believer today be any different from that of a believer before the crucifixion? How can the Christian community encourage those who are suffering? Would this encouragement look any different or be any more effective (if at all) than what a non-Christian support group could provide?

26

—o—

WHAT'S IN A NAME?

The Israelites are stubborn,
like a stubborn heifer.
—HOSEA 4:16

Understandably, our sensibilities might cause us to wince a bit when we encounter Hosea's use of strongly pejorative similes, such as the one in 4:16, in his ultimately futile efforts to persuade Israel to acknowledge and turn from their recalcitrant behavior. His language registers low on the political correctness meter. But by this point in the history of Israel, God's patience with his people has been stretched to the limit, surely warranting some harsh language like this. Israel has persistently ignored their relational responsibilities to their covenant God until the situation has come to a point where he could rightly say, "There is no faithfulness, no love, no acknowledgment of God in the land" (4:1). Through his prophet Hosea, God has been doing everything possible to break through his people's concrete complacency so that they might turn from their sin and experience the blessing he desires for them. And sometimes tough love calls for some tough words.

Even though we might initially have a negative visceral reaction to the words the prophet Hosea uses in 4:16, at least they do not seem to present us with any insuperable difficulties in understanding, much less any apparent surprising significance. But there is much more to this verse than meets the eye of those whose Bible reading is limited to an English translation. That is not to say that the Bible is hiding a secret message here, as though there is some sort of coded communication whose meaning can be found only by those initiated into the mysterious complexities of the Hebrew language, a message that is somehow at odds with the one we read in English. Unsurprisingly, an investigation of our verse in its original language does not uncover any new or different meaning than the one we read in translation. What such an investigation does reveal, however, is a hidden *depth* of meaning that when brought to light will enhance our understanding and appreciation of the prophet's message. In the case of 4:16, the hidden, deeper significance of the prophet's message is found in his use of wordplay, which unfortunately rarely survives the process of translation from one language to another.

Hosea is a master literary craftsman, and Hebrew words are the brushstrokes he uses to create his masterpieces. One technique he often employs in his prophecy is playing on the meaning and the sound of personal names. One illustration of this is his brilliant repurposing of the letters that form the name Ephraim (often used as another name for Israel). In Hebrew, the name Ephraim consists of five consonants:' (א), *p* (פ), *r* (ר), *y* (י), and *m* (מ). Hosea cleverly uses these same consonants throughout his prophecy to form other Hebrew words that highlight the nation's stubborn, rebellious tendency and consequent fruitlessness. So, for example, in 8:9 he uses three of these letters in comparing Israel to a "wild donkey" (פרא *p-r-ʾ*) wandering alone, insisting on going its own way. In 9:16 he again uses three of these letters to depict Israel as a blighted and withered plant that produces no "fruit" (פרי *p-r-y*). In 11:3, he uses all five of the letters (with an extra one thrown in) to describe Israel as a nation that has forgotten that God is the one "who healed them" (רפאתים *r-p-ʾ-t-y-m*).

In 4:16, the verse we're investigating more closely in this chapter, Hosea repurposes two letters of Ephraim's name in describing Israel as a stubborn "heifer" (פרה *p-r-h*). But Hosea's indictment of Ephraim or Israel in this verse by means of wordplay goes even further than this. The word translated as "stubborn," which occurs twice in this verse, has two forms in Hebrew that both share the *s* and *r* sounds: *sōrērâ* (סֹרֵרָה) and *sārar* (סָרַר). These same sounds also appear in the Hebrew word translated as "Israelites": *yiśrāʾēl* (יִשְׂרָאֵל). Not only is there great similarity in the sound of these Hebrew words because of their shared consonants, but in this verse Hosea cleverly places these words right next to each other (in Hebrew, unlike what we encounter in English translations) so that recognition of their similarity is unavoidable: *sōrērâ sārar yiśrāʾēl* (סֹרֵרָה סָרַר יִשְׂרָאֵל).

Hosea's masterful wordplay accomplishes two related things for anyone who hears or reads his prophecy in Hebrew. First, these words of God, delivered through his prophet Hosea, are a catchy and memorable sobriquet that succinctly captures the essential problem with his people: they are so stubborn! Throughout their existence as a nation—a nation chosen by God out of all the nations of earth and called to be identified by their covenant relationship with the one true God—they have consistently refused to follow the direction of God. Hosea prophesies near the time of the collapse of the Northern Kingdom of Israel (722 BC). Yet even at this perilous time, when the nation is in extremis, they continue to stubbornly refuse to listen to their God. Israel (*yiśrāʾēl*) surely deserves the moniker "stubborn" (*sōrērâ/sārar*)! Applying this term to Israel is analogous to calling a thief named Robert "Robbing Robbie" or labeling a callous person named Harold "Hard-Hearted Harry." The nickname captures the essential character of the one named, while using some of the same letters in their name to do so.

But there is a second thing we can say about the masterful wordplay Hosea employs in this verse. By using some of the same sounds found in the Hebrew name "Israel" to describe an essential characteristic of that nation (i.e., stubbornness), Hosea is suggesting that this stubbornness is inherent in Israel itself— that is, the impossibility of even saying the word "Israel" without incorporating the consonants and sounds of the Hebrew word for "stubbornness" implies that the stubbornness is part of the DNA of Israel. It is almost the same as saying that without stubbornness there would be no Israel—that's how ingrained and integral stubbornness is to their very nature. What a clever and powerful way Hosea uses even the consonants of his prophecy to emphasize its content!

It is necessary for us to consider such literary artistry in Hosea's prophecy within its larger context in order to feel the full force of its power. In the book of Hosea, by means of Hosea's on-again, off-again relationship with his unfaithful wife Gomer, God illustrates the unfaithfulness of his own relationship partners, the people of Israel. Anyone reading the sordid account of Israel's infidelity to their covenant relationship with God would have to conclude that the judgment God threatens is indeed deserved. Stubbornness does, in fact, seem to be part of his people's spiritual DNA. They refuse to turn away from their unfaithfulness to God no matter what he says or does. There appears to be as much hope for salvaging God's relationship with his people as there does for salvaging Hosea's relationship with Gomer, described as "a promiscuous woman" and "an adulterous wife" (1:2). Against the dark background of this bleak picture Hosea has painted with his words, however, he splashes some contrasting color. He makes the startling revelation that despite Israel's inherent and intractable stubbornness and deserved judgment, amazingly God has chosen to love them anyway:

> "How can I give you up, Ephraim?
> How can I hand you over, Israel? . . .
> My heart is changed within me;
> all my compassion is aroused." (11:8)

Hosea's brilliant and repeated wordplay involving Israel's stubbornness, then, serves to spotlight not only the utter unworthiness of the one loved but also the relentless love of the lover! Astonishingly, God does not abandon his people in the midst of their stubborn sin. Instead, he inexplicably maintains his steadfast love toward them. Many years later, the apostle Paul would make it clear that the stubborn sinfulness we encounter in Hosea's prophecy characterizes both Jews and non-Jews. Indeed, all of us are like Israel as depicted by Hosea. We are all inherently stubborn and rebellious and are completely dependent on the unmerited grace of God for any hope of redemption. In the words of Paul, "There is no difference between Jew and Gentile, for all have sinned and fall short of the glory of God, and all are justified freely by his grace through the redemption that came by Christ Jesus" (Rom 3:22–24). So there is reason for hope in this seemingly hopeless situation. The stubborn sin of Jews and gentiles is overwhelmed by the even more stubborn grace of God. Hosea's wordplay on the rebelliousness of Israel by which he depicts them as a stubborn heifer leads inexorably to the graciousness of God depicted as a self-sacrificial lamb.

THINGS TO CONSIDER

1. Through his prophet Hosea, God gave his people a nickname that captured the essence of their character. What nickname do you think captures the essence of the character of God's people today? What nickname do you think captures the essence of your own relationship with God?

2. Do you think God's relentless love obviates the requirement of judgment that sin and rebellion merit? Hosea was speaking to the Northern Kingdom of Israel in the days right before they were conquered and exiled by Assyria. How does God's continued love for his people square with what they experienced?

3. Even though God, through Hosea's prophecy, made it abundantly clear that he was aware that "stubbornness"

and "Israel" are almost synonymous terms, he nevertheless reasserted his continued love for them. How does this
kind of love differ from contemporary understandings of
love? As the Holy Spirit transforms Christians to be more
like Jesus, what should this kind of love look like in us?

27

—o—

NOMEN EST OMEN

Tell it not in Gath . . .
—Micah 1:10

I n the United States, as perhaps in every country, there are
  towns whose names are either strikingly appropriate or inappropriate, considering their circumstances. Inappropriate town
names include, for example, the infamous Money, Mississippi.
This dying town is hardly what one would think of as affluent.
According to Wikipedia, "It has fewer than 100 residents, down
from 400 in the early 1950s when a cotton mill operated there."[1]
Another example is Hell, Michigan, where one might expect the
weather to be downright toasty. But on January 8, 2014, its temperature plummeted to -4°F (with a windchill of -27°F).[2] On the
other hand, some town names seem very appropriate. One hardly
needs much imagination to correctly guess the reason for the
names of Seaside, Florida, or Mountain View, Colorado.

A clever writer could have a field day with these names. We encounter such a clever writer in the prophet Micah, although his wordplay is hidden behind a language that is foreign to many of us, making his powerful use of town names to give punch to his prophecy seem like nothing more than a collection of seemingly ordinary verses.

Micah prophesied to Israel and Judah sometime between 750 and 686 BC, when they had strayed far from faithfulness to the Lord. Micah was given the unenviable task of prophesying God's judgment "because of Jacob's transgression, because of the sins of the people of Israel" (1:5). And God would use the Neo-Assyrian kings to execute that prophesied judgment. Micah prophesied against these twelve towns[3] in Judah by using words that play on the meaning of their Hebrew names:

1. "Tell it not in Gath" (1:10).

    The command "tell" (תַּגִּידוּ *taggîdû*) contains the consonants of the name Gath (גַת *gat*). How ironic is it that one is not to "tell" about the coming judgment in a town whose name includes the word "tell"! No doubt the directive is intended to keep the inhabitants of Gath, a Philistine city, from hearing about this disaster coming upon God's people and gloating over it (cf. 7:8).

2. "In Beth Ophrah roll in the dust" (1:10).

    A woodenly literal translation of this town's name would be "house of dust." In Israelite culture, covering oneself or sitting in the dust was a sign of grief or mourning (Josh 7:6; Job 16:15; Isa 47:1). This town's name, then, describes an appropriate response to the coming disaster.

3. "Pass by naked and in shame, you who live in Shaphir" (1:11).

   In Hebrew, this town's name means "beautiful" or "pleasant." This is another ironic taunt because the town and its inhabitants will be just the opposite of beautiful or pleasant when judgment comes. The town will be destroyed, and its humiliated and plundered citizens led away into exile.

4. "Those who live in Zaanan will not come out" (1:11).

   "Zaanan" (צַאֲנָן ṣa'ănān) shares consonants with the Hebrew word for "come out" (יָצְאָה yāṣə'â). Instead of doing what their town name suggests (come out), those in Zaanan will stay inside, cowering behind their walls when the enemy comes.[4]

5. "Beth Ezel is in mourning; it no longer protects you" (1:11).

   This town name means something like "house of proximity." Its presence would be reassuring to any neighbors who might call on it for help. But in the day of judgment, that help would no longer be available.

6. "Those who live in Maroth writhe in pain, waiting for relief" (1:12).

   "Maroth" (מָרוֹת mārôt) sounds like the Hebrew word for "bitter" (מָרָה mārâ). The devastation they would experience would indeed be a bitter pill to swallow.

7. "Disaster has come from the Lord, even to the gate of Jerusalem" (1:12).

   "Jerusalem" is the Hebraization of a name found in early Akkadian texts as URU salīm, meaning "city of peace."[5] When "disaster has come . . . even to the gate of" the city of peace, then the situation is bleak indeed!

8. "You who live in Lachish, harness [to] fast horses . . . the chariot" (1:13).

"Lachish" (לָכִישׁ *lākîš*) sounds like the Hebrew for "to fast horses" (לָרֶכֶשׁ *lārekeš*). Even though the people of this town might try to escape the impending doom by the fastest transportation available, their efforts would be in vain.

9. "You will give parting gifts to Moresheth Gath" (1:14).

"Moresheth" (מוֹרֶשֶׁת *môrešet*) sounds like the Hebrew word for "possession" (מוֹרָשָׁה *morāšâ*). Instead of counting this town as one of its possessions, the kingdom of Judah would have to send it away with parting gifts as one would send away a bride to a groom. In this case, the very scary groom would be the Neo-Assyrian king Sennacherib!

10. "The town of Akzib will prove deceptive to the kings of Israel" (1:14).

"Akzib" (אַכְזִיב *'akzîb*) means "deceptive (thing)" (אַכְזָב *'akzāb*). Any help expected from this town will prove to have been deceptive after it falls to the invading Assyrians.

11. "I will bring a conqueror against you who live in Mareshah" (1:15).

"Mareshah" (מָרֵשָׁה *mārēšâ*) sounds like the Hebrew word for "conqueror" (יֹרֵשׁ *yōrēš*). Once again, the name of the town portends its future. The town that has the word "conqueror" within it will indeed have a conqueror within it!

12. "The nobles of Israel will flee to Adullam" (1:15).

"Adullam" (עֲדֻלָּם *'ădullām*) may be related to Semitic

roots meaning "to lock in" (Akkadian *edēlu*) or "to turn aside" (Arabic عَدَلَ *'adala*). If the nobles of Judah do seek to turn aside from the conflict and lock themselves into this town as some sort of refuge, they will be disappointed. Adullam is the place where David fled to escape King Saul, who sought his life (1 Sam 22:1). Now, at the end of the monarchy, the remaining nobles will flee to the same place in a vain attempt to escape Sennacherib, who seeks their lives.

Micah's play on these names reflects the idea expressed by the Latin phrase *nomen est omen* ("the name is a sign"). With impressive literary skill, Micah demonstrates that the names of these twelve towns are certainly signs of the judgment God would bring against his unfaithful people. But surprisingly, Micah's prophecy does not end with judgment. Micah continues to play with names, this time his own name, to describe something entirely unexpected and unmerited that God would do after the coming judgment:

> Who is a God like you,
>> who pardons sin and forgives the
>> transgression
> of the remnant of his inheritance?
> You do not stay angry forever
>> but delight to show mercy.
> You will again have compassion on us;
>> you will tread our sins underfoot
>> and hurl our iniquities into the depths of the sea.
>> (Mic 7:18–19)

Micah's longer name in Hebrew is מִיכָאֵל (*mîkā'ēl*), which means "Who is like God?"—exactly the question Micah asks at the beginning of the passage just cited. The answer, of course, is no one! No other God is as merciful and compassionate. And every time people would mention Micah's name, they would be reminded of that fact, even in the midst of experiencing their well-deserved judgment.

Micah foresees God's mercy and compassion not only in regard to his historical people after the judgment they would experience at the hands of the Assyrians but also in regard to the future in which a *name* will again be highlighted:

> "But you, Bethlehem Ephrathah,
>> though you are small among the clans
>>> of Judah,
>> out of you will come for me
>>> one who will be ruler over Israel,
>> whose origins are from of old,
>>> from ancient times." . . .
> He will stand and shepherd his flock
>> in the strength of the LORD,
>> in the majesty of the *name* of the LORD
>>> his God.
> And they will live securely, for then his greatness
>> will reach to the ends of the earth.
>>> (5:2, 4; italics added)

Seven hundred years later, the magi recognized the fulfillment of this prophecy in the birth of the Messiah (Matt 2:6). And the *name* of the Messiah is again significant. The angel of the Lord appeared to Joseph and told him, "You are to give him the name Jesus, because he will save his people from their sins" (1:21). Indeed, the name Jesus is the Greek form of the Hebrew name יְהוֹשׁוּעַ (yəhôšûaʿ or Joshua) and means "the LORD saves."

Like the towns in Micah's prophecy, Jesus "lived into" the meaning of his name. He accomplished salvation for his people, and now his name is exalted and commands worship:

> Therefore God exalted him to the highest place
> and gave him the name that is above
> every name,
> that at the name of Jesus every knee should bow,
> in heaven and on earth and under the earth,
> and every tongue acknowledge that Jesus Christ
> is Lord,
> to the glory of God the Father. (Phil 2:9–11)

In the seemingly ordinary verses of Micah's prophecy, we found remarkable significance to the names of the towns listed. And the significance of names in Micah's prophecy points toward the significance of the name of the One who would bring forgiveness and blessing on the other side of the judgment those town names portended. The New Testament leaves no doubt who that One is. The name of each town in Micah's prophecy foreshadowed a future that was either ironically contrary or strikingly appropriate to the meaning of its name. Believers take the Lord's name for themselves by calling themselves Christians. Will future generations look back on us and find that name to be ironic or appropriate? Will the expression *nomen est omen* be true for us?

THINGS TO CONSIDER

1. Does God still judge his people as he did in Micah's day? Have his standards changed? Does the judgment Jesus experienced on behalf of believers change the dynamic of judgment? If so, how?

2. Micah prophesied hope at the same time he prophesied judgment. The towns he listed would all experience hard times before they would see any deliverance. Consider how this historical situation foreshadows Jesus's crucifixion. How might Micah's twofold prophecy be reflected, for example, in Jesus's words at the Last Supper: "This cup is the new covenant in my blood, which is poured out for you" (Luke 22:20)?

3. Micah 4:5 says, "All the nations may walk in the name of their gods, but we will walk in the name of the LORD our God for ever and ever." Considering what you read in this chapter, what do you think it means to "walk in the *name* of the LORD"?

2 8

—o—

Nowhere to Run,
Nowhere to Hide

The river gates are thrown open
and the palace collapses.
It is decreed that Nineveh
be exiled and carried away.
Her female slaves moan like doves
and beat on their breasts.
Nineveh is like a pool
whose water is draining away.
"Stop! Stop!" they cry,
but no one turns back.
—Nahum 2:6–8

Not only is the deeper meaning of Nahum 2:6–8 hidden to English readers, but the very location of the book in which these verses are found is also a mystery to many Christians! It is tucked away in the far corner of the Old Testament in the middle of the Minor Prophets, a section of Scripture seldom visited by Bible readers, preached on by ministers, or selected by small group leaders as a topic for Tuesday morning Bible study.[1] Adding to the problem is the fact that the biblical book of Nahum is not even found in most historical and contemporary lectionaries (i.e., the schedules of biblical passages to be read during worship services). No doubt passages such as the one above from Nahum have contributed to this neglect. After all, what possible relevance could Nineveh have for us today? Who cares about what happened to it so long ago? Answering these questions reveals a surprising significance to these seemingly ordinary verses that has lain hidden in plain sight for so long.

In its day, Nineveh was a magnificent and fearsome city. It was the royal capital of the Assyrian Empire, and as already discussed (see ch. 12), that empire was infamous for its horrifying treatment of all who stood in the way of its rabid ambition to dominate the world. This ambition led, unfortunately, to frequent and devastating confrontations with God's people.

Around 743 BC, the mighty Assyrian king Tiglath-Pileser III exacted tribute from King Menahem of Israel, amounting to about thirty-eight tons of silver (2 Kgs 15:19–20). But this was just the beginning. During the reign of King Pekah of Israel (738–732 BC), Tiglath-Pileser returned to the promised land and "took Gilead and Galilee, including all the land of Naphtali, and deported the people to Assyria" (15:29). After this humiliating episode, the Bible reports that Hoshea son of Elah "conspired against Pekah [the king of Israel] . . . attacked and assassinated him, and then succeeded him as king" (15:30). Tiglath-Pileser's own records indicate that he was the one who "installed Hoshea" as Israel's king, helping us understand how an assassin could end up ruling the kingdom of his victim. But this too came with a hefty price tag. Israel was forced to pay the king of Assyria about seven hundred and fifty pounds of gold and perhaps as much as thirty-eight tons of silver.[2] But the respite from Assyrian bullying that this payment bought was short-lived. When Shalmaneser V, the successor to Tiglath-Pileser, "discovered that Hoshea was a traitor" and no longer paid him tribute, Shalmaneser "seized him and put him in prison. . . . [Then he] invaded the entire land, marched against Samaria and laid siege to it for three years. In the ninth year of Hoshea, [Shalmaneser's successor, Sargon II] captured Samaria and deported the Israelites to Assyria" (2 Kgs 17:4–6). What an ignominious end to the Northern Kingdom of Israel!

And the Southern Kingdom of Judah did not escape Assyrian molestations either. King Ahaz had actually been so foolhardy as to invite Tiglath-Pileser to help him with his opposition to an Israel-Syria alliance. Of course, Tiglath-Pileser was more than happy to oblige him—at a cost. Ahaz "took the silver and gold found in the temple of the LORD and in the treasuries of the royal palace and sent it as a gift to the king of Assyria" (16:8). But King Hezekiah, the son of Ahaz, chose faithfulness to the Lord over faithfulness to Assyria. Consequently, Hezekiah was attacked by Sennacherib, a later king of Assyria who "attacked all the fortified cities of Judah and captured them" (18:13). Though Hezekiah was able to prevent him from destroying Jerusalem through the payment of tribute, the reprieve from Assyrian aggression was brief. Sennacherib later once again threatened

Jerusalem and was turned back only by a divine intervention in which "the angel of the LORD went out and put to death a hundred and eighty-five thousand in the Assyrian camp" (19:35). (See ch. 12.)

Assyria had terrorized its ancient Near Eastern neighborhood, repeatedly attacked God's people, humiliated their king, plundered their resources, and had sent families and friends into exile. It is no wonder, then, that a prophetic message announcing the downfall of this dreaded bellicose behemoth would be welcomed enthusiastically by its many victims, including the people of God. And it is the thoroughness of that divine judgment that is underscored by the *form* of this passage. Certainly, the *content* clearly communicates the watery destruction of Nineveh, the capital city. But the words used in the original language add even more force to the pronouncement. That hidden depth of meaning can be accessed with a basic understanding of Hebrew verbs.

Unlike English, Hebrew has seven verb stems. Each of these verb stems nuances the verb's main meaning to indicate how the action or state communicated by the verb is taking place. So the *qal* verb stem indicates simple direct action (e.g., he *kicked* x); the *niphal* verb stem indicates simple passive or reflexive action (e.g., he *was kicked* or he *kicked himself*); the *hiphil* verb stem indicates that someone or something is causing the action (e.g., he *caused* x *to kick* y); the *hophal* verb stem indicates that the action is being caused (e.g., he *was caused to kick* x); the *piel* verb stem indicates that someone or something is causing a state (e.g., he *caused* x *to sleep*); the *pual* verb stem indicates that a state is being caused (e.g., he *was caused to sleep*); and the *hithpael* verb stem indicates that a state is being reflexively caused (e.g., he *caused himself to sleep*). This is an oversimplification of a complex verbal system, but grasping the precise nuances of these individual verb stems is not crucial for understanding the hidden depths of meaning in our passage. What *is* important to realize is that Hebrew uses seven verb stems to describe all the different kinds of actions or states possible.

We can begin to understand how powerful a statement God is making, therefore, when we notice that he uses six of the seven available Hebrew verb stems in the course of just three verses! Nahum 2:6–8 is one of the most verb-stem-rich contexts in all of the Old Testament. It is as though God has chosen to use almost every Hebrew verb stem that exists to communicate the fact that his judgment against Nineveh will involve every kind of action possible (italics added):

> The river gates *are thrown open* [*niphal* stem]
>> and the palace *collapses* [*niphal* stem].
> It *is decreed* [*hophal* stem] that Nineveh
>> *be exiled* [*pual* stem] and *carried away*
>> [*hophal* stem].
> Her female slaves *moan* [*piel* stem] like doves
>> and *beat* [*piel* stem] on their breasts.
> Nineveh is like a pool
>> whose water *is draining away* [*qal* stem].
> "*Stop! Stop!*" [*qal* stem] they cry,
>> but no one *turns back* [*hiphil* stem].

In other words, there is no escape for Nineveh from God's judgment. There is nowhere to run and nowhere to hide. It is coming at them in every way possible and from all directions. The divine judgment involves active, passive, reflexive, and causative activity—a dire reality communicated by the multiplicity of verb stems employed to describe it.

The English translations of this passage clearly communicate the inevitable and total downfall of Nineveh. But reading this passage in Hebrew and recognizing the multiple verb stems with which the narrator has taken pains to describe Nineveh's end enables the reader to grasp more deeply the breadth, the certainty, the awesomeness, and the awfulness of that end—in other words, to realize more fully what a dreadful thing it is to fall into the hands of the living God (Heb 10:31).

THINGS TO CONSIDER

1. It would have been hard for an Israelite to believe that their tiny nation would outlast the seemingly invincible Assyrians, who had pushed them around for so many years. Yet God had set a limit to their depredations, and he would ultimately remove Assyria from the world stage. What seemingly invincible enemies are you facing? Do you believe God is in control of them?

2. Nahum's name means "comfort" or "comforted" in Hebrew. Does it comfort you to know that one day God will judge all those who oppose him and his people? If so, do you feel guilty for deriving comfort from that knowledge?

3. The Bible says that Christ died for sinners (Rom 5:8) and the unrighteous (1 Pet 3:18), in other words for those who oppose God and his people. But we have received forgiveness and comfort from God instead of the judgment we deserved. How do these truths motivate us to pass this forgiveness and comfort on to others (2 Cor 1:4)?

29

—o—

LEX TALIONIS

*Who has not felt
your endless cruelty?*
—NAHUM 3:19

E arlier, in chapter 12, we saw how horribly the Neo-Assyrian
Empire treated anyone who dared to oppose them. It would
have appeared to any objective observer that this cruel empire
could do as it pleased with the nations of the world. And as we
have seen in the preceding chapter, the prophecy of Nahum
foretells the coming divine judgment against this international
terror. This news would surely be welcomed by the entire world
community, and to some extent expected by Nahum's people.
After all, the holy and righteous God is the judge of all the earth
(Gen 18:25). So it is not surprising to read in Nahum's prophecy
that God would finally put an end to Assyria's cruelty. But what
is surprising is the deeper meaning that lies buried in the last

verse of this prophetic book (Nah 3:19). It is hidden behind layers of language and history that obscure nuances and richness from our understanding of the prophet's message. In this chapter, we'll remove those layers one at a time so that the full power and justice of God's actions can be seen.

The first layer obscuring an additional insight into Nahum's prophecy consists of the clever use of a single Hebrew word. But to remove this layer, we first need to be reminded of an important principle of biblical law (and, indeed, a principle that should govern any sound legal system)—the principle of equity. This principle simply means that the punishment should correspond in severity to the crime it addresses. For example, anyone with a healthy sense of justice and equity would consider it wrong to sentence a serial killer to only two months of community service. It would be equally wrong to sentence someone who stole a pack of gum from the neighborhood convenience store to twenty years in prison. No, we expect the severity of the penalty for breaking a law to be consistent with the severity of the offense. There should be recognizable proportionality or balance between the crime and its punishment. In the more academic language that deals with biblical law, this is referred to as the *lex talionis*—a Latin term meaning "law of retaliation." Although this unfortunate term may suggest an officially sanctioned vengeance or brutality, its purpose "was to secure as exact an equation as is humanly possible between crime and punishment."[1]

This principle of proportionality is articulated in three passages of the Old Testament (Exod 21:23–25; Lev 24:19–20; Deut 19:19–21), with the first containing its fullest expression: "If there is a serious injury, you are to take life for life, eye for eye, tooth for tooth, hand for hand, foot for foot, burn for burn, wound for wound, bruise for bruise." While such language may seem harsh to our modern sensibilities, it ensures not only equitable punishment for wrongdoers but also that the punishment does not go too far. It must correspond as closely as possible to the crime.[2] So what does this principle have to do with our passage? And how is it hidden behind the clever use of a Hebrew word?

To answer these questions, we must first allow that God's judgment of this sinful nation would have to correspond to his own guidelines for judging, which include the principle of proportionality; the punishment must fit the crime. But how does the principle of proportionality apply to "endless cruelty"? The Hebrew root of the word translated as "endless" in our passage is עבר ('-b-r). The general meaning of this root is "to pass over, pass by."[3] When used to describe Assyria's cruelty, it implies a malicious brutality that has exceeded (i.e., passed over) all boundaries of acceptable conduct. In contemporary idiom, we would describe their behavior as "beyond the pale." What would be the appropriate judgment for a crime that has exceeded all bounds? The answer lies unseen at the other end of this prophetic book. When we go back to the first chapter, we find that the author has already answered this question, but his answer is hidden to those who read his words only in English translation.

In Nahum 1:8, the prophet describes the punishment God would bring against Assyria's crime. The first half of the verse states, "With an overwhelming flood he will make an end of Nineveh." This statement is usually understood figuratively to refer to the divine judgment that would overflow the nation's capital in the form of an invading army that would "make an end" of it. But there is deeper meaning here. The Hebrew adjective Nahum uses to describe the flood is intentional and powerfully significant. It is formed from the same Hebrew root we already encountered at the very end of the book: עבר (ʿ-b-r). By using the same Hebrew root, Nahum underscores the fact that Assyria would receive precisely what it deserves. Divine judgment against Assyria would *pass over* or *overwhelm* them because their cruelty had *passed over* or *overwhelmed* everyone else. This is a classic application of the *lex talionis*: "eye for eye"—and, we would add, עבר for עבר—and is in accordance with the words Jesus spoke on a mountainside over six hundred years later: "In the same way you judge others, you will be judged, and with the measure you use, it will be measured to you" (Matt 7:2). Assyria had judged others with "endless cruelty," so they would receive the "overwhelming flood" of divine judgment. Perfect justice.

A second layer obscuring a fuller appreciation of our passage involves a bit of history. As we saw above, the term *overwhelming flood* is usually understood figuratively as referring to an opposing army that imposes a judgment so decisive and encompassing that it is unstoppable and inescapable. But there is some historical evidence that the term here can also be understood literally as referring to onrushing floodwaters that "pass over" their normal channels. The ancient Greek historian Diodorus Siculus, who lived in the first century BC, recounts details surrounding the fall of Nineveh in book 2 of his *Library of History.* Interestingly, in his account he notes that the Assyrian king at the time, Sin-shar-ishkun (referred to as Sardanapallus by Diodorus), was aware of an ancient prophecy that "no enemy will ever take Ninus [i.e., Nineveh] by storm unless the river shall first become the city's enemy."[4] In other words, it would take an "overwhelming flood" of the kind the prophet Nahum described. And that is exactly what Sin-shar-ishkun experienced in 612 BC, when after a two-year siege by a military alliance consisting of Medes, Babylonians, and others, the walls of Nineveh were finally breached and the city was overrun. Diodorus provides us with the details:

> But in the third year, after there had been heavy and con-tinuous rains, it came to pass that the Euphrates [*sic*, Tigris], running very full, both inundated a portion of the city and broke down the walls for a distance of twenty stades [i.e., about 2.25 miles]. . . . The rebels, on learning of the death of Sardanapallus [i.e., Sin-shar-ishkun], took the city by forcing an entrance where the wall had fallen.[5]

Whether this surging of the Tigris was naturally occur-ring or the result of a deliberate manipulation of the irrigation system,[6] the *overwhelming flood* of the Tigris River allowed an *overwhelming* attacking force to *flood* into the capital city of Nineveh, laying it waste in 612 BC and precipitating the demise of the Neo-Assyrian Empire only a few years later in 609 BC, after the fall of its last stronghold in Harran. So, both literally and figuratively, Nineveh was destroyed by an "overwhelming flood" of both opposing forces and the waters of the Tigris.

Nahum's message is clear to all, even with the layers of a foreign language and the dust of history obscuring its depth. But when these are removed, the substance and rationale for the prophecy come into much sharper focus. God would justly destroy Nineveh with an overwhelming flood because of their overwhelming cruelty. The appropriateness of this divine judg-ment is indicated by the same Hebrew root word being found at both the beginning and the end of the book, a literary device called an *inclusio*, bracketing the entire composition and highlighting its content—a literary feature hidden beneath translations of the Hebrew. And a bit of history unknown to most readers reveals a literal overflowing that incarnates the divine judgment. That incarnated judgment would ultimately be fulfilled by Jesus Christ, of course. He would experience the full, overwhelming judgment of God against not only Nineveh's overwhelming sin but ours as well.

THINGS TO CONSIDER

1. The form of Nahum's prophecy has been carefully constructed to reflect the *lex talionis*, the principle of proportionality between an offense and its punishment. What do you think would be a proportional punishment for the offenses you've committed in your life? Do you think eternal punishment is proportional?

2. Through our faith in Jesus, God forgives our guilt and does not punish us as our sins deserve. Is this a violation of the principle of proportionality? Jesus was perfectly obedient to the Father's will and yet was crucified for our sins. How does this fit with the principle of proportionality? Or doesn't it?

3. In Matthew 5:38–42, Jesus seems to turn the principle of proportionality on its head. He says,

You have heard that it was said, "Eye for eye, and tooth for tooth." But I tell you, do not resist an evil person. If anyone slaps you on the right cheek, turn to them the other cheek also. And if anyone wants to sue you and take your shirt, hand over your coat as well. If anyone forces you to go one mile, go with them two miles. Give to the one who asks you, and do not turn away from the one who wants to borrow from you.

How does the fact that our overwhelming sin has been paid for by Jesus's death (his experience of overwhelming judgment) on our behalf change the calculation of the principle of proportionality?

30

—o—

FAMILY RESEMBLANCE

Has not the one God made you? You
belong to him in body and spirit. And what
does the one God seek? Godly offspring.
So be on your guard, and do not be
unfaithful to the wife of your youth.
—MALACHI 2:15

Located near the end of the Old Testament, Malachi 2:15 lies within a context full of challenges. Indeed, biblical scholars are in general agreement that "these verses are certainly the most problematic in Malachi."[1] Making sense of Malachi 2:15, therefore, will not be an easy task. Thousands of years of history and thousands of miles of geographical separation from the original time and place in which these prophetic words were uttered have obscured their intended meaning from contemporary readers.

This is another one of those biblical passages, then, that we're interested in exploring further!

Apart from some further investigation, the middle two clauses of our verse appear to have the prophet Malachi calling for the multiplication of children among God's people or, though more difficult to understand, some sort of divine offspring. But, as we will see, what the prophet is communicating here refers to neither of those things. But like a rare coin lying hidden among the other coins in our pocket, the true meaning of these words lies hidden among the words that surround it. We will be able to discern the deeper meaning of our verse only by going through those surrounding words carefully.

The key to understanding the surprising significance of this seemingly ordinary verse lies in the frequent occurrence of the word "one" in this verse and in earlier verses in the same chapter. If we expand our field of vision to include the larger context of our verse (2:10–16), we discover the word "one" used no fewer than four times to describe God (italics added):

Do we not all have *one* Father? (2:10)
Did not *one* God create us? (2:10)
Has not the *one* God made you? (2:15)
And what does the *one* God seek? Godly offspring. (2:15)

What an unusual adjective for the prophet to use to describe God! Of course, there is only one true God, but the Bible rarely describes God by using the word "one" in this way. In fact, the two verses in Malachi cited previously are the only times in the entire Old Testament where God is referred to as "one God" or "one

Father." Perhaps God is not usually described as "one" because it is so obvious and central to the biblical testimony.[2] So Malachi must be using the word here to stress something that is not so immediately obvious. To understand this less obvious emphasis of Malachi, we have to broaden our perspective to include all of his prophecy. Only by means of this broader perspective will we be able to discern how the strange words of our verse fit into the larger message he's delivering to God's people.

Like most biblical prophets, Malachi was not called to an easy task. He was sent to speak to a dispirited and discouraged group of people. These people had returned to the promised land after decades of exile in Babylon during which their children had grown and had children of their own. These next generations had heard the stories of Israel's glory in the past. We can only imagine their great expectations as they rebuilt the temple and the walls surrounding Jerusalem. After these significant accomplishments, they had waited patiently for God to restore their status and prestige among the nations to what it had been before, to what they had heard their parents and grandparents describe. The years passed, and they continued to wait . . . and wait. But nothing happened. When Malachi spoke to these people, they had been waiting for over a hundred years for God's glory to be manifest in their midst once again! It isn't hard to imagine that doubts had begun to creep into their theology: doubts about their status as God's chosen people, doubts about God's forgiveness of their sin, doubts about God's continuing interest in them. Some had begun allowing for the possibility that God had given up on them. They thought it just might be the case that God didn't love them anymore. If that were true, then did it make any sense to continue to serve him? Maybe their commitment to him was misplaced.

Their doubts about God's continuing love and commitment to them inevitably began to affect their love and commitment to him. So God sent the prophet Malachi to remind his people of some important truths about who God is and who his people should be.

Malachi begins his message by reminding God's people of his special love for them: "'I have loved you,' says the LORD" (1:2). God specifically chose them out of all the nations of the earth to be the objects of his affection. And this special choice should color everything about them—that is, they should be people who reflect the attributes of the God they worship. They should, in effect, manifest by their lives the same spiritual DNA of the author of life with whom they were in such a close relationship. Most of the book of Malachi explains what this should look like among God's people. God is honorable, worthy of honor, so his people should behave honorably themselves and give God the honor he is due (1:6–2:9). God is characterized by justice, so his people should behave justly toward one another (2:17–3:5). It is God's nature to give, so generosity, not stinginess, should also characterize his people (3:6–12). God is trustworthy, so his people should serve him with humble trust (3:13–15). Family members will have some resemblance to each other. So those who are the people of God should have some resemblance to him.

Now that we have some orientation to what Malachi's prophecy is all about, we're ready to give 2:15 another look. This verse appears in a passage that also addresses how the way God's people live should reflect something true about God himself. As we have seen, in 2:10–16, four times God is described as "one." The rarity of this expression makes it clear that an emphasis is being placed on the unity of God. Every other time Malachi emphasizes some attribute of God, he does so to stress how that attribute should also characterize God's people. Keeping this in mind enables us to comprehend the greater depth of meaning in our verse.

In 2:10–16, some behaviors of God's people that are undermining their unity are described. These include "marrying women who worship a foreign god" (2:11) and divorce (2:14–16).

It is impossible for the people of God to retain their distinctiveness when their loyalty to God, their commitment to his service, and their unity of purpose are being diluted by those who possess none of those traits—that is, by those who worship foreign gods. Moreover, the truth about God should not simply be communicated vocally by his people but also visually. The truth about God emphasized in our verse is that God is a unity, he is *one*. So his people should be characterized by unity as well. And this unity should be most evident in the closest human relationship possible—the marriage relationship. But the fact that husbands were being unfaithful to their wives, and subsequently divorcing them, was communicating to those outside the community of God's people exactly the wrong thing about God. In other words, by their *dis*unity, God's people were bearing false witness about God himself. Now the deeper meaning of our passage is clear. Malachi is communicating God's will that his people should live in a way that manifests the truth about him. Malachi 2:15 can be paraphrased as, "Because God, who is a *unity*, made you, and because your lives should be being conformed to his likeness, he seeks people who by their *unity* with one another (especially in the marriage relationship) demonstrate his *unity*. These are his true children."

About four and a half centuries later, Jesus would pray for the same thing to be true of his followers—not surprising since

God never changes, and Jesus is God incarnate. Before he was arrested, Jesus spent an extended time in prayer. After praying for his disciples, Jesus prayed for all believers, emphasizing again the importance of their unity, with God and with one another:

> My prayer is not for them alone. I pray also for those who will believe in me through their message, that *all of them may be one*, Father, just as you are in me and I am in you. May they also be in us so that the world may believe that you have sent me. I have given them the glory that you gave me, that *they may be one as we are one*—I in them and you in me—so that *they may be brought to complete unity*. Then the world will know that you sent me and have loved them even as you have loved me. (John 17:20–23; italics added)

Jesus makes it clear in his prayer before his crucifixion, that he wants his own unity with the Father to be visually communicated by the unity of his followers with one another. God continues to seek children who communicate the truth about him with their lives, and especially by their unity.

THINGS TO CONSIDER

1. Does your life reflect God's spiritual DNA? Can people recognize in you, a child of God, any attributes of your Father? Jesus said, "Anyone who has seen me has seen the Father" (John 14:9). What kind of person do people see when they look at you?

2. What area of your life or personality most clearly reflects to others something true about God? What area of your life or personality may lead others to conclude something untrue about God?

3. What does the fragmentation of the Christian church communicate to unbelievers about the God we claim to serve? Does Christian unity trump theological orthodoxy? How does a believer decide what theological or social issues are worth compromising the truth about the unity of God?

Select Bibliography

Astour, Michael C. "Ugarit and the Great Powers." Pages 3–29 in *Ugarit in Retrospect: 50 Years of Ugarit and Ugaritic.* Edited by Gordon D. Young. Winona Lake, IN: Eisenbrauns, 1981.

Belibtrou, Erika. "Grisly Assyrian Record of Torture and Death." *BAR* 17.1 (1991): 52–61, 75.

Bruckner, James. *Jonah, Nahum, Habakkuk, Zephaniah.* NIVAC. Grand Rapids: Zondervan, 2004.

Budge, E. A. Wallis. *The Teaching of Amen-Em-Apt, Son of Kanekht.* 1924. Repr., Whitefish, MT: Kessinger, 2010.

The Compact Oxford English Dictionary. Oxford: Clarendon, 1991.

Diodorus Siculus. *Library of History.* Translated by C. H. Oldfather. 3 vols. LCL. Cambridge: Harvard University Press, 1933–1939.

Feinberg, Charles L. "Jeremiah." Pages 357–691 in vol. 6 of *EBC.*

Finkelstein, J. J. "Ammiṣaduqa's Edict and the Babylonian Law Codes." *JCS* 15 (1961): 91–104.

Grisanti, Michael A. "Deuteronomy." Pages 457–814 in vol. 2 of *EBCr.*

Leemans, W. F. "The Rate of Interest in Old-Babylonian Times." *RIDA* 5 (1950): 5, 7–34.

McCarthy, D. J. *Treaty and Covenant: A Study in Form in the Ancient Oriental Documents and in the Old Testament.* 2nd ed. AnBib 21A. Rome: Biblical Institute Press, 1978.

Moscati, Sabatino, ed. *An Introduction to the Comparative Grammar of the Semitic Languages.* Wiesbaden: Harrassowitz, 1980.

Nevres, M. Özgür. "20 Amazing Hurricane Facts." *Our Planet—Pale Blue Dot.* September 8, 2019. https://ourplnt.com/hurricane-facts/#axzz6KpB3rmE5.n

Schuller, Eileen M. "The Book of Malachi." Pages 843–77 in vol. 7 of *NIB.*

Scurlock, J. A. "The Euphrates Flood and the Ashes of Nineveh (Diod. II 27.1–28.7)." *Historia* 39 (1990): 382–84.

Sparks, Kenton L. *Ancient Texts for the Study of the Hebrew Bible: A Guide to the Background Literature.* Peabody, MA: Hendrickson, 2005.

Waltke, Bruce K. *Genesis: A Commentary.* Grand Rapids: Zondervan Academic, 2001.

Waltke, Bruce K., and O'Connor, M. *Introduction to Biblical Hebrew Syntax.* Winona Lake, IN: Eisenbrauns, 1990.

Westbrook, Raymond, and Roger D. Woodard, "The Edict of Tudhaliya," *JAOS* 110 (1990): 641–59.

Westermann, Claus. *Genesis 1–11: A Commentary.* Translated by John J. Scullion. Continental Commentaries. Minneapolis: Augsburg, 1984.

Williams, Michael. *Hidden Prophets of the Bible: Finding the Gospel in Hosea through Malachi.* Colorado Springs, CO: Cook, 2017.

———. *How to Read the Bible through the Jesus Lens: A Guide to Christ-Focused Reading of Scripture.* Grand Rapids: Zondervan Academic, 2012.

———. "Taking Interest in Taking Interest." Pages 113–32 in *Mishneh Todah: Studies in Deuteronomy and Its Cultural Environment in Honor of Jeffrey H. Tigay.* Edited by Nili Sacher Fox, David A. Glatt-Gilad, and Michael J. Williams. Winona Lake, IN: Eisenbrauns, 2009.

Notes

CHAPTER 1: ONE OF THESE THINGS IS NOT LIKE
THE OTHERS
1. Jacobus van Dijk, "Myth and Mythmaking in Ancient Egypt," in
   CANE, 3:1699.
2. Ibid.
3. Ibid.
4. "From Papyrus Bremner-Rhind," trans. James P. Allen (*COS*
   1.9:14).
5. Dijk, "Myth and Mythmaking in Ancient Egypt," 1700.
6. "Epic of Creation," trans. Benjamin R. Foster (*COS* 1.111:391).

CHAPTER 2: MADE FOR EACH OTHER
1. Don McMinn, "Details Are Important," *Reflections on Life and
   Leadership* (blog), November 27, 2018, https://donmcminn.com
   /2018/details-are-important/.
2. *HALOT* 2:811–12; BDB, 740; *NIDOTTE* 3:378–79.

CHAPTER 3: AN EYE-OPENING EXPERIENCE
1. *COED*, 469.
2. Bruce K. Waltke and M. O'Conner, *Introduction to Biblical
   Hebrew Syntax* (Winona Lake, IN: Eisenbrauns, 1990), 265
   (§14.4e, #15).
3. *HALOT* 3:988–89.

4. *HALOT* 2:817–20.

CHAPTER 4: RECOGNIZING "RECOGNIZE"

1. Joseph was seventeen years old when his brothers sold him into slavery (Gen 37:2). He subsequently spent some time (of unknown duration) in service to Potiphar, and over two years in prison (41:1), so that "he was thirty years old when he entered the service of Pharaoh" (41:46). He subsequently served seven years as Pharaoh's second-in-command during the years of plenty and presumably at least a couple of years during the famine (41:53) before his brothers made the trip to Egypt for grain. Thus, Joseph would have been around thirty-nine years old when he saw his brothers again.

2. One could even argue for four times if the narrator's use of a homonym in 42:7 is counted: "he pretended to be a stranger [וַיִּתְנַכֵּר *wayyitnakkēr*, from the (different) root נ-כ-ר]."

3. Cf. Michael Williams, *How to Read the Bible through the Jesus Lens: A Guide to Christ-Focused Reading of Scripture* (Grand Rapids: Zondervan Academic, 2012), 13.

CHAPTER 6: IMAGE PROBLEMS

1. They nevertheless arrive at the same number of *ten* commandments by splitting what is usually numbered as the tenth commandment into two: one commandment prohibiting coveting a neighbor's wife and one prohibiting coveting anything else.

2. Unless combined with the first (as in the Roman Catholic and Lutheran traditions), in which case it would be the longest commandment.

3. Walter C. Kaiser Jr., "Exodus," in *EBC*, 1:480.

4. Consider, for example, Bruce K. Waltke, *An Old Testament Theology* (Grand Rapids: Zondervan, 2007), 469, who says: "From Aaron's viewpoint it was merely a matter of iconography, representing God by a bull and in that way holding 'a festival to [the Lord]' (Exod 32:5)."

5. Erik Hornung, "Ancient Egyptian Religious Iconography," in *CANE*, 3:1713.

6. Bruce K. Waltke, *Genesis: A Commentary* (Grand Rapids: Zondervan Academic, 2001), 65, italics added.

7. Claus Westermann, *Genesis 1–11: A Commentary*, trans. John J. Scullion, Continental Commentaries (Minneapolis: Augsburg, 1984), 158.

CHAPTER 7: GRACE IN PLACE

1. "The Laws of Eshnunna," trans. Martha Roth (*COS* 2.130:333), §6.

2. "The Laws of Hammurabi," trans. Martha Roth (*COS* 2.131:350), §259.

3. "The Middle Assyrian Laws," trans. Theophile J. Meek (*ANET*, 187), §§C8, F1.

4. "The Laws of Hammurabi," *COS* 2.131:350, §253.

5. Cf. "The Laws of Hammurabi," *COS* 2.131:337–38, §§7, 9–11, 22.

6. See Michael J. Williams, "Taking Interest in Taking Interest," in *Mishneh Todah: Studies in Deuteronomy and Its Cultural Environment in Honor of Jeffrey H. Tigay*, ed. Nili Sacher Fox, David A. Glatt-Gilad, and Michael J. Williams (Winona Lake, IN: Eisenbrauns, 2009), 124.

7. W. F. Leemans, "The Rate of Interest in Old-Babylonian Times," *RIDA* 5 (1950): 18, italics added.

8. Williams, "Taking Interest," 125.

CHAPTER 8: ENDURING WITNESSES

1. For a more detailed account of these people, see J. G. Macqueen, *The Hittites and Their Contemporaries in Asia Minor* (London: Thames & Hudson, 1986).

2. See, for example, the discussion by Michael A. Grisanti, "Deuteronomy," in *EBCr*, 2:462–63. See also D. J. McCarthy, *Treaty and Covenant: A Study in Form in the Ancient Oriental Documents and in the Old Testament*, 2nd ed. (Rome: Biblical Institute Press, 1978), 51–85.

3. Cf. 4:45, which begins with "These are the stipulations . . ."

CHAPTER 9: BE CAREFUL WHAT YOU ASK FOR

1. Raymond Abba, "Name," *IDB* 3:501. See also Leland Ryken, James C. Wilhoit, and Tremper Longman III, eds., "Name," *DBI*, 582–83.

CHAPTER 10: AROUND THE GLASSY SEA

1. M. Özgür Nevres, "20 Amazing Hurricane Facts," *Our Planet— Pale Blue Dot*, September 8, 2019, https://ourplnt.com/hurricane -facts/#axzz6KpB3rmE5.
2. John Monson, "1 Kings," in *ZIBBC*, 3:39.
3. Gwendolyn Leick, "Yam," *DANE*, 325.
4. Ryken, Wilhoit, and Longman, "Sea," *DBI*, 765.
5. Maltbie D. Babcock, "This Is My Father's World," 1901.

CHAPTER 11: THE LAST STRAW

1. Gerald A. Klingbeil, "מַס," *NIDOTTE* 2:992–95 (here, p. 993).
2. See Gösta W. Ahlström, "Administration of the State in Canaan and Ancient Israel," in *CANE*, 1:601–2.
3. *CAD* 10:117.
4. J. J. Finkelstein, "Ammiṣaduqa's Edict and the Babylonian Law Codes," *JCS* 15 (1961): 101.
5. See "The Edict of Ammisaduqa," trans. J. J. Finkelstein (*ANET*, 526–27).
6. Ibid., 526.
7. See Raymond Westbrook and Roger D. Woodard, "The Edict of Tudhaliya," *JAOS* 110 (1990): 641–59.
8. Ibid., 653.

CHAPTER 12: A BIRD IN A CAGE

1. These horrendous acts are spelled out in all their gruesomeness by Erika Belibtrou, "Grisly Assyrian Record of Torture and Death," *BAR* 17.1 (1991): 52–61, 75. This article is available online in pdf format at: http://faculty.uml.edu/ethan_Spanier/Teaching

/documents/CP6.0AssyrianTorture.pdf. Further descriptions of Assyria's atrocities are described by James Bruckner, *Jonah, Nahum, Habakkuk, Zephaniah*, NIVAC (Grand Rapids: Zondervan Academic, 2004) 28–29.

2. "Sennacherib's Siege of Jerusalem," trans. Mordechai Cogan (*COS* 2.119B:303).

3. Ibid., 302–3.

4. "The Babylonian Chronicle," trans. Alan Millard (*COS* 1.137:467–68, Chronicle 1.iii.34–38); and "The Murder of Sennacherib," trans. William W. Hallo (*COS* 3.95:244).

CHAPTER 13: UNFINISHED BUSINESS

1. Anthony Tomasino, "Esther," in *ZIBBC*, 3:486.

2. Mordecai's name appears fifty-six times in English and fifty-eight times in Hebrew. Esther's name appears forty-seven times in English and fifty-five times in Hebrew.

3. Other Amalekites survived as well. See 1 Sam 27:8; 30:1, 18; 2 Sam 1:8, 13: 8:12; 1 Chr 4:43.

4. Through fasting and prayer (4:16). Although prayer is not explicitly mentioned, it usually accompanied such fasting (cf. 2 Sam 12:16; Neh 1:4; Dan 9:3).

CHAPTER 14: THE CLOUD RIDER

1. Amarna letter EA 45. Cf. Michael C. Astour, "Ugarit and the Great Powers," in *Ugarit in Retrospect: 50 Years of Ugarit and Ugaritic*, ed. Gordon D. Young (Winona Lake, IN: Eisenbrauns, 1981), 16.

2. Cf., e.g., *CTA* 5.vi.10; 6.iii.1, 3, 9, 21; 6.iv.29, 40.

3. Gerald L. Mattingly, "Baal," *DANE*, 41–42. See also Michael David Coogan, *Stories from Ancient Canaan* (Philadelphia: Westminster, 1978), 116.

4. "The Ba'lu Myth," trans. Dennis Pardee (*COS* 1.86:260).

5. "The Ba'lu Myth," *COS* 1.86:262.

6. Cf., e.g., *CTA* 2.iv.28–29; 4.iii.10; 4.v.120–21; 5.ii.6–7.

7. Cf. Sabatino Moscati, ed., *An Introduction to the Comparative Grammar of the Semitic Languages* (Wiesbaden: Harrassowitz, 1980), 25: "Interchanges between the consonants of the bilabial group [i.e., *b* and *p*] . . . take place in several [of the Semitic] languages."

CHAPTER 15: HERE THERE BE DRAGONS

1. "The Ba'lu Myth," *COS* 1.86:265.
2. Ibid., 1.86:252.
3. A slight variation occurs in Ezek 32:2, where instead of *tannîn* we find *tannîm*, but this is no doubt a simple confusion of the *-în* ending of *tannîn* with Hebrew masculine plural ending *-îm*.

CHAPTER 16: STREET SMARTS

1. *HALOT* 3:989; BDB, 834; *NIDOTTE* 3:714–16.
2. John Newton, "Amazing Grace," 1779.

CHAPTER 17: WE'VE GOT YOUR NUMBER

1. *COED*, 1584.
2. For more on the symbolic meaning of numbers, see Ryken, Wilhoit, and Longman, "Numbers in the Bible," *DBI*, 599–600; and Marvin H. Pope, "Number, Numbering, Numbers," *IDB* 3:561–67.
3. Daniel D. Luckenbill, *Ancient Records of Assyria and Babylonia*, 2 vols. (Chicago: University of Chicago Press, 1927), 2:65.
4. Cf. Williams, *How to Read the Bible through the Jesus Lens*, 78–81.

CHAPTER 18: DIVINE DESIGN

1. "Instruction of Amenemope," trans. Miriam Lichtheim (*COS* 1.47:116).
2. Ibid., §I:5–6.
3. For even more parallels, see Kenton L. Sparks, *Ancient Texts for the Study of the Hebrew Bible: A Guide to the Background Literature* (Peabody, MA: Hendrickson, 2005), 71.

4. Miriam Lichtheim, *AEL* 2:147.

5. Sparks, *Ancient Texts for the Study of the Hebrew Bible*, 70.

6. Tremper Longman III, "Proverbs," in *ZIBBC*, 5:497.

CHAPTER 20: THE DEATH OF DEATH

1. See, for example, chs. 10 and 14.

2. "The Ba'lu Myth," *COS* 1.86:266.

3. John Donne, Sonnet X ("Death Be Not Proud"), *John Donne: The Major Works*, ed. John Carey (Oxford: Oxford University Press, 2000), 175–76.

CHAPTER 22: BREAK TIME

1. "Execration Texts," trans. Robert K. Ritner (*COS* 1.32:50).

2. Steven Voth, "Jeremiah," in *ZIBBC*, 4:279.

3. "The Execration of Asiatic Princes," trans. John A. Wilson (*ANET*, 329).

4. Ibid.

5. Georges A. Barrois, "Hinnom, Valley of the Son of," *IDB* 2:606.

6. See, for example, Matt 5:22, 29–30; 10:28; 18:9; 23:15, 33; Mark 9:43, 45, 47; Luke 12:5; Jas 3:6.

CHAPTER 23: THE DESIGNATED DRINKER

1. Cf. also Pss 16:5; 116:13.

2. Consider also Isa 51:17, 22; Jer 49:12; Lam 4:21; Ezek 23:31–33; Zech 12:2.

CHAPTER 24: THE BIGGER THEY ARE

1. Charles L. Feinberg, "Jeremiah," in *EBC*, 6:535.

2. Paul S. Minear, "Babylon (NT)," *IDB* 1:338.

CHAPTER 27: *NOMEN EST OMEN*

1. Wikipedia, s.v. "Money, Mississippi," last modified April 4, 2022, https://en.wikipedia.org/wiki/Money,_Mississippi.

2. Charlie Campbell, "It's Official: Hell Has Frozen Over," *Time*,

January 8, 2014, https://nation.time.com/2014/01/08/its-official
-hell-has-frozen-over/. We will avoid here the obvious jokes
about hell freezing over.

3. The following explanation of the wordplay involving these
   town names is drawn in large measure from Michael Williams,
   *Hidden Prophets of the Bible: Finding the Gospel in Hosea through
   Malachi* (Colorado Springs, CO: Cook, 2017), 111–13.

4. This imagery is taken from Bruce K. Waltke, "Micah," in *A
   Commentary on Obadiah, Jonah, Micah, Nahum, Habakkuk,*
   vol. 2 of *The Minor Prophets: An Exegetical and Expository
   Commentary,* ed. Thomas Edward McComiskey (Grand Rapids:
   Baker Academic, 1993), 628.

5. See Chris Hays, "Akkadian Loanwords and Wordplays in Isaiah,"
   in *Basics of Akkadian: A Complete Grammar, Workbook, and
   Lexicon,* by Gordon P. Hugenberger with Nancy Erickson (Grand
   Rapids: Zondervan Academic, 2022), 153–54.

CHAPTER 28: NOWHERE TO RUN, NOWHERE TO HIDE

1. For the continuing significance of the Minor Prophets for
   believers today, see Williams, *Hidden Prophets of the Bible.*

2. "Summary Inscription 4," trans. K. Lawson Younger, Jr. (*COS*
   2.117C:288). In the inscription, the amount of the silver to be
   paid as tribute is unclear.

CHAPTER 29: *LEX TALIONIS*

1. J. A. Motyer, "Civil Law and Justice in Biblical Times," *EDT*, 247.

2. For more discussion, see Bruce Wells, "Exodus," in *ZIBBC*,
   1:238–39.

3. *HALOT* 2:778–80; BDB, 716–19; *NIDOTTE* 3:314–16.

4. Diodorus, *Library of History,* 2.26.9 (Oldfather, LCL).

5. Diodorus, *Library of History* 2.27.1–2 (Oldfather, LCL).

6. For a discussion of the various possibilities, see J. A. Scurlock,
   "The Euphrates Flood and the Ashes of Nineveh (Diod. II
   27.1–28.7)," *Historia* 39 (1990): 382–84.

CHAPTER 30: FAMILY RESEMBLANCE

1. Eileen M. Schuller, "The Book of Malachi," in *NIB*, 7:864.

2. Consider, e.g., the words of the Shema, a central confession of the Jewish faith repeated at least twice daily in morning and evening prayers: "Hear, O Israel: The LORD our God, the LORD is one" (Deut 6:4).

How to Read the Bible through the Jesus Lens

A Guide to Christ-Focused Reading of Scripture

Michael Williams

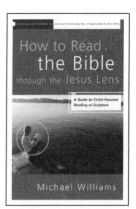

If you sometimes feel as if the Bible teaching you receive comes as small puzzle pieces you don't know how to fit together, this book is for you. All these pieces connect in Christ to form a coherent picture, and author Michael Williams shows you how in this tour of each book of the Bible.

In addition to showing how relevant each biblical book remains today, Williams enlivens other Christian disciplines such as Bible reading, Scripture memory, and evangelism. An excellent tool for Bible teachers, ministry leaders, and students, *How to Read the Bible through the Jesus Lens* is an invaluable guide for reading, studying, and understanding the entire Bible.

> "Few books do a better job of giving us an overview of Genesis to Revelation in such a compact way. This is the sort of book I'd love to have in the hands of every member of my church!"
> —Justin Taylor, managing editor, ESV Study Bible

> "[Offers] suggestive and stimulating ways for us to see Christ as the climax of the story; let Williams begin to shape the way you read the whole Bible."
> —Kelly M. Kapic, professor of theological studies, Covenant College

> "Michael Williams has written a book that is badly needed: a survey of all the books of the Bible that shows how they work together to point toward Jesus Christ... accessible to almost any reader."
> —Douglas J. Moo, Wessner Chair of Biblical Studies, Wheaton College

ZONDERVAN®
.com

NIV Study Bible

*Dr. Ken Barker; Mark Strauss;
Jeannine Brown; Craig Blomberg;
Michael Williams*

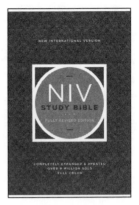

Set in Zondervan's exclusive NIV Comfort
Print typeface, this stunning, full-color study
Bible answers your pressing questions with
just the right amount of information, placed
in just the right location.

With its decades-long legacy of helping readers grasp the Bible's
meaning, the *NIV Study Bible* embodies the mission of the NIV translation to be an accurate, readable, and clear guide into Scripture.
Specifically designed to expand on the NIV, the *NIV Study Bible*'s edi-
torial team crafts that same accuracy and clarity into every study note.

Features:

- Complete text of the world's bestselling modern-English Bible
  translation, the New International Version (NIV)
- Over 21,000 bottom-of-the-page study notes, with icons to
  make information easy to spot
- Over 125 topical articles, 16 pages of full-color maps, the
  comprehensive NIV Concordance with nearly 4,800 word
  entries, and a notes index enable even deeper study
- 66 book introductions and outlines along with 6 section
  introductions provide valuable background information for
  each book of the Bible
- In-text maps, charts, diagrams, and illustrations visually clarify
  the stories in the Bible
- Words of Jesus in red
- Exclusive Zondervan NIV Comfort Print typeface
- 9-point print size